THE STRUGGLE OF İBRAHİM:

Biography of an Australian Muslim

THE STRUGGLE OF İBRAHİM:
Biography of an Australian Muslim

Salih Yücel

New Jersey

Published by Tughra Books

345 Clifton Ave., Clifton,

NJ, 07011, USA

www.tughrabooks.com

Library of Congress Cataloging-in-Publication Data Available

ISBN: 978-1-59784-225-9

Printed by

Çağlayan A.Ş., Izmir - Turkey

CONTENTS

INTRODUCTION

İbrahim Hussein Dellal is a leading Muslim figure in the post-World War II Australian Muslim community. The National Archives of Australia describes İbrahim as an enthusiastic community leader and philanthropist in "Uncommon Lives: Muslim Journeys", compilation of material devoted to the history of Muslims in Australia. He has been active in the state of Victoria, starting with his role in bringing Turkish immigrants to Australia and facilitating their settlement. He has a hand in many firsts in the Victorian Muslim community, making him a pioneer in educational institutions and religious organizations.

İbrahim been linked to Muslim history through lineage. He is the grandson of the last Ottoman mufti of Cyprus, Sheikh Mehmed Aal. The mufti was second in charge after the governor, acting as a supreme judge and heading religious affairs.

Born in 1932 in Larnaca, Cyprus, İbrahim was surrounded by with Turks, Greeks, Armenians, Jews and Arabs. He was exposed to the mix of faiths and cultures that continues to enrich Cyprus. Growing up in harmony with people of different faiths and cultures gave rise to his love of humanity and belief in coexistence.

Religion and spirituality were like the blood running in the veins of İbrahim's family. Children were named after prophets or relatives of the prophets. In a household where religious education began early, children understood the necessity of a higher purpose. At the age of five, İbrahim and his brother saw a vision of themselves in the sky building a mosque in a beautiful country. This vision would come true in 2001 in Australia.

İbrahim's parents, especially his mother, raised their sons to be *Osmanli Efendisi*, an Ottoman gentleman. He was raised to be loyal to his faith and dedicated to his community. The world and all of its inhabitants belong to God, and hence need to be honored and protected. A human's duty is to serve others, regardless of differences, through good endeavors and kind acts.

He attended the American Academy, a Baptist missionary school, and graduated from the British Technology Institute, both in Cyprus. The influence of his Western education clashed at times with his traditional upbringing based on Islam, service, and Turkish patriotism.

İbrahim emigrated to Melbourne, Australia, in 1950, following his brothers, in search of a better life. There were few Muslims and no Islamic organizations and mosques in Melbourne. İbrahim was still a young man, adapted to the dominant Western culture and lifestyle. It was not until 1956 when İbrahim met with more Muslims that he returned to his spiritual and cultural roots. Together with the passion instilled in him by his parents and the efforts of the local Muslims, including leading Muslims of Victoria, such as Sheikh Fehmi al-Imam and Dr. Abdul Khaliq Kazi, İbrahim established or assisted with the establishment of many religious, educational, and cultural organizations, holding major roles in each:

- Cypriot Turkish Society (1956)
- Islamic Society of Victoria (1957)
- Preston Mosque (1962)
- Australian Federation of Islamic Societies (AFIS) (1964)
- Coburg Mosque (1971)
- Thomastown Mosque (1972)
- Western Thrace Society and Prahran Mosque (1974)
- Australian Federation of Islamic Councils (AFIC) (1976)
- Halal Meat Committee (Chairman) (1976)
- Cypriot Turkish Islamic Society (1986)
- Selimiye Foundation (1991)
- Işık College (seven campuses in Victoria) (1997)
- Sunshine Mosque (2001)

Due to their roles in establishing the first permanent Muslim organizations, Sheikh Fehmi and Dr. Kazi are also essential figures in Australian Muslim history deserving biographies of their own. While, Sheikh Fehmi's ability to draw from his memories has greatly weakened, Dr. Kazi has contributed to this biography.

In his earlier years in Victoria, İbrahim encountered the grandchildren of the last Afghan camel riders and Muslim immigrants who arrived after the First World War. He eagerly listened to their stories and orally transmitted them to the Muslims who would arrive in later years. He wanted to keep their stories alive because of their contribution to mapping the Australian terrain in the mid-nineteenth century.

He played a major role in the late 1960s in bringing Turkish immigrants to Australia and in helping them to settle in their new homeland. Moreover, İbrahim made substantial contributions to Australia, founding numerous organizations and earning Australia billions of dollars through the export of *halal* (Islamically permissible) meat to Muslim countries. His contributions led to him being awarded the Silver Jubilee Medal by Queen Elizabeth in 1977. In 2007, İbrahim's name appeared on the Queen's Birthday Honors List as a Member in the General Division of the Order of Australia.

Throughout his years of leadership and representation of Muslims in Australia, İbrahim met with prominent political and religious leaders, such as Iranian spiritual leader, Great Ayatollah Khomeini, Indonesian president, Abdurrahman Wahid, Australian Prime Minister, Kevin Rudd, Turkish Prime Minister, Tayyip Erdogan, head of the Ministry of Religious Affairs of the Turkish Republic, Tayyar Altıkulaç, global Sufi leader, Sheikh Nazım al-Qubrisi, and global Turkish Muslim spiritual leader, Fethullah Gülen.

Due to his involvement in formation of the *halal*[1] meat industry and expansion to an export trade, he had opportunities to meet with

---

[1] Halal means anything permissible in Islam. In reference to foods, Islam has laws regarding which foods can be consumed, and regulations on the slaughter of animals for consumption. For example, pork and alcohol are not halal, and so is not

ministers in Australia, Indonesia, Iran, Algeria, Saudi Arabia, Kuwait, and the United Arab Emirates.

İbrahim's meeting with Turkish scholar and global spiritual leader, Fethullah Gülen, in 1991 was a focal point in his life. Gülen was the inspiration that İbrahim had been seeking for many years. He internalised Gülen's views on education and community service through compassion. To him, Gülen is a contemporary Jalal ad-Din Rumi, a 13th century Muslim mystic whose poems on love and spirituality are among the most read in the Unites States. Henceforth, İbrahim committed himself to educating Muslim youth.

İbrahim's love of community service had been instilled in him by his parents while being raised in the multi-faith mix of Cyprus. To serve the community was a source of honour and pride for his family due to the emphasis of service in Islam, where it is perceived as a form of worship, and in Turkish culture, where it is a fundamental value. The culture of service and hospitality is the legacy of İbrahim's parents. İbrahim has taken this on as his inheritance, and has made it his life's work. For İbrahim, serving others is an act of worship. After he encountered the Gülen Movement, a global faith-based educational movement, his love for giving and working for others developed even further, especially in the field of education.

Not all agreed with İbrahim's actions and views. He was criticized by some Muslim community leaders and members and accused of being an opportunist and hypocrite. Yet his gentle nature and dislike of conflict prevented him from even responding. İbrahim is a man who prefers to slowly build trust and he treats others with compassion. It is due to these characteristics that there are so many who admire and love him.

In his seventies, he still does not consider retiring from his volunteer work. Despite the fact that he officially retired in 1991 from the telecommunication industry, he continues to work as a volunteer

---

consumed. Animals that are not slaughtered according to Islamic regulations are also not considered halal.

six days a week. The thought of decreasing the time he spends helping others does not appeal to him. "If I don't do this, I will die. It is a part of my life, and I will do this until my last breath," he said. He prays twice a day to God, asking God to lengthen his life and grant him health so that he may continue to serve the various communities in Australia. He added, "If I had one more life to live, I would use it to appeal to wealthy persons and try to convince them to spend their entire wealth on educating lower-class children." İbrahim believes that "a peaceful society and a good economy are based on a good education with moral values."

There is a part of İbrahim, specifically spiritual life, that will remain a mystery. As is the habit of many pious and sincere individuals, İbrahim hesitated to reveal this side of himself, not only out of humility, but also out of fear of being misunderstood. I persuaded him to provide at least some insight into this area in order to help future generations to see that there is another dimension that inspires his community activism and struggle. Judging by his tone and words, I feel that the little that he did reveal to me was only the tip of the iceberg.

Married to an Irish-Australian woman and the father of three daughters, İbrahim still lives in Victoria and continues to serve the community primarily through education and interfaith dialogue. He has long since devoted himself to the Australian community through volunteer work.

The idea of writing this book came when I traveled with İbrahim to Canada and the United States for a retreat and an academic conference. Through our conversations over the 10-day trip, I discovered that İbrahim was "a living history" of the Australian Muslim community. He had witnessed the growth of the Muslim population and struggles to settle and integrate into Australia. His memory was weakening due to old age, so it was essential that his precious experiences with Australia's Muslims were documented for the benefit of Australia and Australian Muslims.

İbrahim was very happy with the idea of a biography because he hoped future generations would remember and understand the difficulties and joys experienced by Muslims who established organizations, and built mosques and educational institutions in Australia.

I began interview sessions with him, and contacted him many times through phone calls to ask for dates or missing information. I arranged interviews with his family members, relatives, close friends, and colleagues. Together, we made visits to significant historical sites. He let me review his collection of pictures, newspaper clippings, letters, official documents, and video clips. I perused through local ethnic and national newspapers for mention of İbrahim.

Readers will find the stories from his community efforts to be fascinating, and, at times, humorous, and his various experiences to be treasures of wisdom. Within these pages, the politicians and spiritual leaders that İbrahim admires and interacted with are named, and the organisations İbrahim dedicated himself are listed. This book will be of interest to all Australians, young and old, because his life is a success story, not in terms of wealth, but in contributions to the community. İbrahim lived in Australia, but his memories are an inspiration to anyone, anywhere who seeks to read a fascinating life story.

I offer my sincere gratitude to İbrahim. He patiently answered my enquiries as I prodded him for details. I would also like to thank his family, relatives, close friends, and colleagues for further enhancing the portrait of İbrahim presented in the following pages. I would like to express my appreciation to İbrahim, Dr. Abdul Khaliq Kazi, and Asiye Aceyoğlu for providing pictures.

CHAPTER 1

İbrahim's Roots

İBRAHİM'S ROOTS

THE SICK MAN OF EUROPE IS DYING

I brahim can trace his genealogy in Cyprus to the mid-nineteenth century, the era of the Ottoman Empire's decline. His family was among the respected Ottoman families in Cyprus, and remained as a noble family after the annexation of Cyprus by the British Empire in 1878.

In the late nineteenth century, the Empire was affected by economic troubles, social unrest, and ethnic rebellions. The great Empire which used to be a leading economic and political power, lost its power after Europe prevailed with the Industrial Revolution. The Empire's budget deficit was huge and the Ottoman state could not repay the lending nations. Attempts at financial reform failed to revitalize the Empire's economy. European nations were enjoying a period of economic prosperity due the technological advancements that occurred during the Industrial Revolution.

The sultanate was losing its soft power over its territory and allies, and its military weakened due to being behind technologically. Nationalists in the Arab nations rose against Ottoman officials and engaged in guerrilla warfare. Egypt was attempting to sever its ties with the dying Empire.

After three centuries of Ottoman control, Cyprus had been taken over by the British Empire. The Greeks, Bulgarians, Albanians, and Bosnians within the Empire rebelled as nationalistic influences were on the rise. The Armenians, who were once called *Milleti Sadika*, "Loyal Nation", were aided by Russia and received weapons to fight against the Ottoman army, and nationalist Turks and Kurds. The

Ottomans' military power was insufficient to cope with the European states due to general conditions within the Empire[2].

There was disunity, arguments, and betrayals among Ottoman paşa's (generals), governors, religious leaders, and corrupt local authorities contributed to the unrest. Public trust was diminishing towards the state and judicial system. Nationalistic movements and philosophy brew ethnic divisions in the intellectual community.

There were two major groups fighting for power within the Ottoman Empire: *Ittihat ve Terakki Cemiyeti* (The Committee of Union and Progress or CUP) and Pan-Islamists. The CUP was pro-Western and in favour of reforming administration and educational systems within the Empire. It was lead by secularists who wanted to separate religion and state and some ultra-secularists who wanted to eradicate any political relation with religion. Even within the groups, there were major divisions. The CUP included communists, republicans, and those who wanted to retain the sultanate but with limited power. Another subgroup was the pan-Turks who desired to break off from the non-Turkish nations within the empire, and form a discrete Turkish state.

The second group was the Pan-Islamists who wanted to unite Muslims all over the world against Russia and the European nations[3], the two dominant powers at that time. They were sharply divided into reformists, traditionalists, and Sufis[4]. They failed to accommodate the changes brought on by modernity.

In 1876, Abdul Hamid II was appointed Sultan of the Ottoman Empire. Due to his diplomatic and politics skills (e.g., his effective use of the *Yildiz Teşkilati*, (an intelligence agency that he established) and his support of the Pan-Islamism movement, he was able to slow but not stop the inevitable collapse of the Empire. Pan-Islamism was

---

2   Nuri Cevikel, TTK Belleten (Turkish Historical Society), V72, no.263, April 2008.

3   M. Şükrü Hanioğlu, *The Young Turks in Opposition*, Oxford University Press, 1995, p. 17

4   Sufism is the mystical dimension of Islam that focuses on spirituality and love of God.

the Sultan's principal political strategy for regaining Muslim support and combating internal and external threats to the Ottoman Empire[5], including European powers who were attempting to re-take Cyprus through the establishment of secret relations with its Christian population[6]. The Sultan did not want to lose Ottoman influence over Cyprus, even though it was annexed by the British Empire in 1878.

The Sultan chose loyal, patriotic, and religious figures and appointed them to critical political and military posts (such as governors, caliphate representatives, army captains, and religious leaders); however, not all remained loyal to him. He trusted them to help him regain Ottoman soft power and strengthen ties between local centres of power and the imperial government. Moreover, he intended to assume a central leadership role within the Pan-Islamic movement.

"The diversionary tactic was partially successful in stimulating Muslim favour against the Christian nationalists within and without the empire."[7] Some imams, Sufi masters, and spiritual leaders throughout the Muslim world began to mention the name of the Sultan during the Friday sermons, even in distant lands outside the Ottoman Empire such as the Philippines and South Africa. For the minority Muslims living in colonized lands, mentioning the Sultan's name was an indication of loyalty to the Empire.

In the late nineteenth century, ethnic nationalism was widespread. There were uprisings by the Albanians, Bosnians, Serbs, Armenians, Greeks, and Arabs living under the control of the Ottoman Empire. The CUP policies reflected a growing Turkish nationalism or pan-Turkism. This sparked reactionary movements, like pan-Arabism. When the Ottoman system and philosophy of *Ummah* (Muslim community) failed to revitalise the Empire, Arab nations turned to unity through language and expanded tribalism.

---

5   Kemal H. Karpat, *The Politicization of Islam*, Oxford University Press, 2001, 148-155.
6   Cevikel 2008.
7   Don Peretz, *The Middle East Today*, Greenwood Publishing Group, CT, USA, 1994, p.71.

Economic conditions within the empire were deteriorating. The central imperial government could not control the provinces. Some local leaders acted autonomously, even to the point of disobeying direct orders from the Sultan. Political corruption was also on the rise as meritocracy decreased. A tax increase led to revolts in Anatolia and other parts of the Empire[8]. Taxes were being improperly used. This resulted in frequent dismissals in judicial and military officials, generating further instability within the government. Moreover, some provincial governors ruled as despots.

Out of fear of civil conflict and war, many farmers abandoned their lands, villages were depopulated, and the Ottoman Empire faced a decline in tax revenues and suffered severe inflation. Due to the war in the Balkans in 1913, there was mass immigration from those areas into Istanbul and neighboring cities. The immigrants faced unemployment, and this led to greater discontent within the empire. European leaders called the Ottoman Empire "the Sick Man of Europe[9]".

The worsening conditions of the Empire and divisions among the intellectual community did not deter İbrahim's family's support of the Sultanate. İbrahim's grandparents raised their children to be loyal to the Ottoman Empire and devoted to Islam. Even though İbrahim was born after the collapse of the Empire and attended an American school, he embraced his Turkish roots.

THE LAST OTTOMAN MUFTI IN CYPRUS

When British governor Lord John Hayes took over the rule of Cyprus from Ottomans, he described the people of Cyprus as follows: "The people are quiet and sociable, very lazy and given pleasures to every short. Robberies, assassinations, and brigandage were nearly unknown,

---

[8]   Anatolia is the name given to the majority of Turkey, which is located on the Asian continent. The area was named Turkey after the collapse of the Ottoman Empire with the signing of the Treat of Lausanne in 1923. In this book, the name "Anatolia" will be used for events occurring before 1923.

[9]   Although it is not clear who first used the name, it first appeared in the *New York Times* on 12 May, 1860.

and drunkenness was not common. The Turkish citizens were devotedly religious[10]."

The British wanted to remove the Turks in power, and increase the population of Greeks, Syrians, Jews, and Arabs to diminish Ottoman influence[11]. Although Cyprus had been incorporated into the British Empire in 1878, the Sultan wanted to retain some influence over the island. Hence, he selected İbrahim's maternal grandfather, Sheikh Mehmed Abdul Aal, to serve as the *mufti* of Cyprus. The Sultan wanted to strengthen the bond between Anatolia and Cyprus through the *mufti*.

Sheikh Aal was an influential Sufi scholar born and raised in Cyprus but with Turkish roots. The family held a degree of influence and respect in Cyprus, making Sheikh Aal an ideal choice for position of *mufti*. The mufti would be put in charge of the *awqaf* [12] (charitable foundations) and religious affairs. Even though the country was under the British rule, religious affairs were left in the authority of the *mufti*.

The role of the *mufti* at that time was to be in charge of all religious affairs in a province and serve as a supreme judge. The *mufti* was second in charge after the governor in a province. The task of last Ottoman *mufti* was not easy and very complicated. All the mosques and awqafs, including religious education and collection and distribution of zakat, were under his responsibility. He was also chief justice

---

10   Panteli, Stavros, (1984) *The New History of Cyprus*, p.53, East-West Publication, London The Hague

11   Panteli, Stavros, (1984) *The New History of Cyprus*, p,48, East-West Publication, London The Hague

12   *Awqaf* means "charitable foundation" that funds schools, hospitals, humanitarian aid, environmental, cultural, and religious organizations. In the 11th century, every Islamic city had at least several hospitals. The *awqaf* trust institutions funded the hospitals for various expenses. The awqaf trusts also funded medical schools, and their revenues covered various expenses such as their maintenance and the payment of teachers, students, and other workers. (Micheau, Francoise, "The Scientific Institutions in the Medieval Near East", pp: 999-1001, in Regis Morelan and Roshdi Rashed, Encylopedia of the History of Arabic Science, pp. 985-1007, vol.3, Routledge, 1996

of the Shariah law court, and dealt with cases of divorce, inheritance, and family disputes.

While the Sheikh was born in Cyprus, İbrahim does not know his maternal grandfather's ethnic background. He assumes that he was Turkish. 'Abdul Aal (or Abdu al Aal) is made up of two words and one article. *'Abd* is the word for "servant" and *ul* or *al* is the article "the". The second *Aal* means family. The Sheikh also spoke Arabic well.

Sheikh Mehmed's mother was a widow with six children who immigrated to Cyprus in the middle of the eighteenth century. Apparently, a wealthy Arab businessman named Kanan supported the family in Cyprus[13]. Kanan may have been a relative since it is Arab custom for the males to take care of female relatives, hence increasing the possibility that the Sheikh had an Arab background. İbrahim does not have information about his great-grandfather or why his great-grandmother immigrated to Cyprus.

It is interesting to note that many members of Sheikh Mehmed's extended family (such as nieces, nephews, and cousins) eventually settled in distant lands including England, America, and Australia, possibly in search of an economically stable life and politically stable country. A few also settled in Anatolia. However, after a while, contact was lost, so it is unclear what happened to most of the distant relatives.

Mehmed Abdul Aal undertook early religious education at the *Hala Sultan Tekke* (Lodge of Hala Sultan). The family ran a livestock trade business with Egypt and Syria. This may have lead to Mehmed studying at Al-Azhar University[14]. Al-Azhar University is the centre of Arabic literature and Islamic sciences. Founded in 975 in Cairo, Egypt, it is the world's second oldest surviving degree-granting university.

After completing his studies at Al-Azhar, Sheikh Mehmed may have travelled to the Balkans and worked for a period of time in reli-

---

13 Iclal Dellal, İbrahim's brother's wife, provided a description of the Dellal family history. Iclal heard this fact from Sheikh Mehmed's younger brother, Haci Mustafa.

14 (Alatas, Syed Farid, 2006. From jami`ah to university: multiculturalism and Christian–Muslim dialogue, *Current Sociology* 54(1) p.112-32

gious affairs, though it is unclear if he was assigned the position. He learned Bosnian and Albanian, interacted with Orthodox Christians, and was comfortable working with individuals possessing differing religious and ethnic backgrounds, making him a suitable choice as Mufti of Cyprus.

Most likely, someone recommended Sheikh Mehmed to the Sultan as capable for various reasons. First, he was a graduate of Al-Azhar University, which was considered a prestigious religious institution. He could speak six languages including Turkish, Arabic, Greek, Armenian, Bosnian, and Albanian. He was familiar with different cultures and faiths having lived in Turkey, Egypt, Cyprus, and the Balkans. Indeed, his family was well established and highly respected in Cyprus. Finally, Sheikh Mehmed was affiliated with a Sufi order, most likely the Naqshbandi[15]. This order has many adherents throughout Cyprus. İbrahim recalls how his grandfather had *murid*s (spiritual wayfarers) who would come to have Sufi lessons with him.

One of Sheikh Mehmed's tasks as mufti was to reduce tensions between different ethnic groups in Cyprus. While the Greeks and Turks were the largest ethnic groups in Cyprus, there were also many Jews, Armenians, and Arabs. Members of the pro-Hellenistic political movement in Cyprus championed the notion that Cyprus joins the Greek nation state, but the British were against it because they wanted to retain control over Cyprus as a colony. Interestingly, the British were interested in establishing a Jewish homeland in Cyprus that would remain under the Empire's power.

---

[15] The Naqshbandi order is a branch of Sufism, the mystical dimension of Islam. It is also notable as it is the only Sufi order that claims to trace its spiritual lineage (*silsilah*) to Prophet Muhammad, peace be upon him, through Abu Bakr, the first Caliph. In contrast, most other orders trace their lineage to Ali, Muhammad's cousin, son-in-law, and the Fourth Caliph. The word Naqshbandi is Persian, taken from the name of the founder of the order, Baha-ud-Din Naqshband Bukhari. (1318-1489). The Naqshbandi Sufi Way, (History and Guidebook of the Saints of the Golden Chain). by Shaykh Muhammad Hisham Kabbani. Kazi Publications, USA 1995).

Through his network of family, friends, Sufis, and business contacts, the Sheikh attempted to establish positive relations with the leaders of other faiths.

The annexation of Cyprus in 1914 enhanced the pro-Hellenistic political movement's influence on the island. The Turks and other Muslim groups opposed the pro-Hellenistic political movement in Cyprus. Indeed, they anticipated more favourable treatment from the British in comparison to the Greeks[16] since the British granted a greater degree of freedom and better economic opportunities.

Even *awqaf* began propagating pro-British views through preachers and the Turkish weekly newspaper, *Hakikat* Newspaper. However, some Turks did not want to live under British rule and they started moving to Anatolia. According to official Turkish government documents, approximately nine thousand Turks left Cyprus by the end of 1924[17].

Sheikh Mehmed was highly respected among Muslims and non-Muslims. He possessed superb language skills which greatly enhanced his ability to effectively work with Muslim and non-Muslim community leaders including Greeks, Armenians, Jews, and Arabs. Despite the bloodshed between different ethnic groups in different parts of the world during the First World War, there were no similar conflicts in Cyprus. Although Turks, Kurds, and Armenians were killing each other in the eastern and southeastern regions of Anatolia, there were no acts of violence in Cyprus. Sheikh Mehmed helped to maintain the peace on the culturally diverse island of Cyprus.

Although Armenians residing in the east and southeast regions of Anatolia were forced by their Ottoman rulers to leave their homes and settle in Lebanon and Syria, nothing like this occurred in Cyprus. According to İbrahim, his grandfather would continuously meet and

---

16   Panteli, Stavros, (1984) The New History of Cyprus, East-West Publication, London
     The Hague p.120
17   *Journal of Cyprus Studies* 14.34 (Jan 2008): p. 5 (46)

consult with Armenian, Jewish, and Greek leaders to avoid conflicts and maintain a peaceful coexistence.

In 1923, the Ottoman state collapsed. The new Turkish Republic embraced strict secular principles. The new government persecuted many religious leaders, Sufi leaders, and clerics in Turkey and banned Sufism and closed almost all Sufi lodges since most were against a secular republic. Furthermore, the government attempted to persecute Sheikh Mehmed in Cyprus; however, Armenians and other prominent families in Cyprus who had established good relations with the new leadership in Ankara, the capital of the Turkish republic, helped prevent the persecution. This clearly illustrates the positive relation between İbrahim's grandfather and non-Muslim community leaders in Cyprus.

The *donmehs*[18] (i.e., converts to Islam) had played a crucial role in the political and economic life of the Ottoman Empire and continued to exert influence on the leaders of the recently established Republic of Turkey. It is possible that Cypriot Armenian politicians contacted Armenian converts in Ankara and asked them to intercede on Sheikh Mehmed's behalf. Indeed, it is also possible that Armenian *donmeh* may have appealed directly to Mustafa Kemal Pasa (Atatürk), the founder of the Republic of Turkey.

Until the British abolished the *awqaf* rules in 1927, the Ottoman and Turkish government would appoint and pay the salaries of clerics. After 1927, British governors appointed these officials and paid their salaries, having more control over the *awqaf* and Islamic clerics. This placed limits on Sheikh Mehmed's activities, making him displeased with British control for the rest of his life. What frustrated Sheikh Mehmed more was the attitude of new Turkish Republic

---

18 Donmeh is Turksih for "to turn". It refers to a believer turning to Islam. Some of the donmeh's were later documented as being Muslim in public, but followed their faiths in private. For more information on donmehs, see J.M. Landau, *The Donmes: Crypto-Jews under the Turkish Rule*, *Jewish Political Studies Review*, 19:1-2 (Spring 2007)

towards religious affairs. They cut administrative and financial support altogether, leaving the *awqaf* to be self-reliant.

Sheikh Mehmed died in 1931, a year before İbrahim was born. However, historical records indicate that a committee of Cypriot Turks elected a new mufti, Hodja Said, in 1931[19]. Hence, it is possible that Sheikh Mehmed died earlier than the aforementioned date.

İbrahim did not see his grandfather, but felt his influence through his mother, Naciye, and through the people who had known Sheikh Mehmed well. Naciye was known by family and friends to be like her father, inheriting his spiritual and moral values. She adopted his passion for caring for the community and devoting her life to pleasing God through worship and righteous behavior. İbrahim remarked, "Whenever I would look at her, I would remember God."

Having a mufti as a grandfather and a pious woman as a mother urged İbrahim to display proper behavior at all times. The community expected İbrahim to behave like his elders, serving others before being served, and acting with respect towards the elderly, being generous when giving, and showing consideration towards the needs of the community. It was an honour to be the grandson of the mufti and a member of the Dellal family, so İbrahim took on his family's way of life. It wasn't until his adolescent years that he began questioning some of the principles he was raised to live by.

İBRAHİM'S PARENTS

İbrahim's maternal grandfather, Sheikh Mehmed, supervised religious affairs in Cyprus. In addition, he was involved in livestock trade with notable people in Egypt, Palestine, and Syria. Sheikh Mehmed worked with İbrahim's paternal grandfather, Hassan Efendi. Hasan Efendi's father, İbrahim's great-grandfather, immigrated to Cyprus from Anatolia. Hassan Efendi was a Turkish livestock trader who had been living in Cyprus for many years.

---

[19] *Journal of Cyprus Studies* 14.34 (Jan 2008): p5(46)

Hassan Efendi and his children Hasan Hüseyin, İbrahim (senior, İbrahim's uncle), Cemaliye, and Hatice underwent a traditional Ottoman upbringing. Hasan Hüseyin named his newborn son İbrahim after the senior İbrahim left Cyprus with his sisters, Hatice and Cemaliye. They moved to south Anatolia to continue their livestock and farm business. The fact that the Dellals had property and business abroad and in Cyprus suggests that they were an established and aristocratic family, or descended from a pasha (Ottoman general). When pashas would be successful after a battle or administrative term, the Sultan would reward them with farmland.

İbrahim's father, Hasan Hüseyin, continued and expanded the trading business after Hassan Efendi passed away. He ended his trading abruptly in 1974 when Turkey invaded Cyprus, and his wife, Naciye, passed away.

Sheikh Mehmed also took care to raise his daughter, Naciye, as a dignified Ottoman lady. He made certain that she married into a noble family. Naciye was known for her wisdom and generosity. Her polite manner and kindness allowed her to get along well with others. Naciye was one of the most respected women in Larnaca. Naciye married Hasan Hüseyin and had three children: Ahmet Mustafa, Hasan, and İbrahim. She greatly desired and prayed to have a daughter as well, but she did not. (PICTURE 1)

CHAPTER 2

Life in Cyprus

LIFE IN CYPRUS

BIRTH OF İBRAHİM

On the 13th of August in 1932, there was excitement in Sheikh Mehmed's son's home. Naciye was taken to the local hospital in Scala near Larnaca and she gave birth to her third son, İbrahim Hussein Dellal. He was the youngest of the three Dellal brothers. When the midwife informed Hasan Hüseyin that the child was a boy, he rejoiced, whereas Naciye was a little less joyful. She had wanted a girl. "All good is from Allah. Boy or girl, it doesn't make a difference," Hasan Hüseyin told those who were there with him.

Hasan Hüseyin came to his wife's bedside. He wished her and the baby well and congratulated her. Both the mother and the baby were in good health. After discussing the naming of the child, they both decided on the name İbrahim for two reasons. First, it was the name of the Prophet İbrahim (Abraham) and it was a family tradition to name children after the prophets, the companions of the prophets, or saints. Second, Hasan Hüseyin's older brother, who was also named İbrahim, had gone to Turkey 16 years ago and perished during the battle at Gallipoli. By naming his son after his brother, Hasan Hüseyin believed that he would keep his brother's memory alive. He thanked his wife for accepting this name. They added the middle name Hussein, name of Prophet Muhammad's grandson, peace be upon him.

Naciye reminded her husband of the tradition of the Prophet regarding newborns. Hasan Hüseyin took the boy in his arms and kissed him for the first time. He then turned towards the *qiblah*, the direction of prayer towards the holy mosque of Ka'bah in Saudi Arabia, and recited the *adhan*, the call to prayer, in the right ear of the baby, followed by reciting the *iqamah*, the second call to prayer, in the baby's left ear. Afterwards, Naciye and Hasan Hüseyin both repeated to the baby, "Your name is İbrahim," three times. Hasan Hüseyin gave his son another kiss and handed him back to his mother saying, "He will be a great man by the grace of God." The parents then both made a short prayer for the baby's health, spirituality, character, and future.

During the first week following İbrahim's birth, Hasan Hüseyin asked one of his workers to sacrifice a sheep or a ram as *aqiqah*. This is also a tradition of the Prophet Muhammad, peace be upon him. The meat was then cooked and served to relatives, neighbors, and the poor and all prayed for the well-being of the newborn in return.

FAMILY BUSINESS

İbrahim's father, Hasan Hüseyin, was a prominent businessman in Cyprus. He would wear an Ottoman *fes* (fez), a *cepken* (a short embroidered jacket with full sleeves), a vest underneath, a *kuşak* (waistband), and *şalvar* (baggy trousers). He also had a handlebar moustache. While some Ottomans would grow beards, İbrahim's father would shave his. His appearance as an Ottoman gentleman was important in his business, both with locals and international merchants. His Ottoman outfit represented loyalty to faith and the Empire, while the embroidering on his jacket marked his class.

Hasan Hüseyin carried on the family business of raising and selling live animals to a number of neighboring countries including Syria, Egypt, Palestine, and other Middle Eastern countries. His customers included wealthy, aristocratic families such as King Farouk Abdullah's cousins in Egypt. With a well-established network of contacts and customers from his father's trading days, the business was thriving under İbrahim's father. His siblings moved to Anatolia where they established a branch of the business and worked with Hasan Hüseyin in Cyprus to satisfy the needs of their customers.

After assigning one of his Arabic-speaking employees to sell animals to Arab countries, Hasan Hüseyin would organize hundreds of sheep, goats, and cows and have them loaded onto cargo boats. Trade was carried out using mostly gold pieces. İbrahim's father trusted his employees. In fact, he did not count the gold pieces his employees received for his livestock.

Hasan Hüseyin workers respected and trusted their employer because he was a man of his word and would show the same level of respect to his workers that he showed to his family. His wife, Naciye, would often prepare food for the workers. Indeed, she would often bake bread and pastries for employees embarking on lengthy business trips for the company.

Despite being poor and uneducated, his employees, whether shepherds or tradesmen would take great care during business negotiations. İbrahim recalled how, after selling livestock, workers would bring gold coins to his mother. She would put the coins away without counting them. İbrahim asked her, "Mother, why don't you count the gold coins they bring?" She replied, "My son, these men have never betrayed us. We trust them completely." İbrahim recalled that "they would bring handfuls of gold coins in purses and my mother would never count them."

İbrahim remains amazed at the trust displayed by both his parents and the workers and wondered how they built this foundation of trust. "My heart longs for those days," he said. The trust between his family and their workers continues to inspire İbrahim. İbrahim observed, "What good days they were. For there to be trust, it is essential that people keep to their word. In our religion, not keeping one's promises has been taken as an attribute of a hypocrite. The secret of success passes through trust." İbrahim often expressed concern about the decrease of trust in the Muslim community and among the Australian people in general.

İBRAHİM'S SPIRITUAL UPBRINGING

İbrahim's mother, Naciye, was a very religious, generous, and spiritual person. She never missed her daily prayers and wore the *çarşaf* (an outer garment covering a woman from head to foot). She would help the poor and needy, and would take special care of the family's workers.

İbrahim's mother was an Ottoman *hanimefendi* (Lady). Although she did not have much formal education, she was an intelligent woman who learned the Qur'an from her parents. Like İbrahim's grandfather, his mother was well respected in Larnaca. She was well known for her kind and amicable character. She embraced all people including members of the non-Muslim community in Cyprus. She maintained friendly relations with the wives of the non-Muslim religious leaders. On occasion they would gather in a religious leader's house and share a meal together. İbrahim would often join her as well. "We were not familiar with discrimination and the notion of 'others' in Cyprus," said İbrahim.

In the Ottoman or Turkish culture, a person demonstrating Naciye's character traits and actions would have been raised in a household that emphasized Sufi principles. Based on the *hadith* of Prophet Muhammad, peace be upon him, the greatest enemy is not another person, but rather the carnal self[20]. This concept dilutes the sense of otherness and leads a person to focus on one's defects. Naciye would tell İbrahim, "My son, everyone is human. Treat them kindly."

According to İbrahim, his mother's self-sacrificing and generous character is reflected in Rumi's famous poem that emphasized the basic principles of humility and selflessness:

> *In generosity and helping others, be like a river.*
> *In compassion and grace, be like the sun.*
> *In concealing other's faults, be like the night.*
> *In anger and fury, be like the dead.*
> *In modesty and humility, be like the earth.*
> *In tolerance, be like the sea.*
> *Either appear as you are, or be as you appear.*

---

20 The Prophet said, "Your greatest enemy is your own *nafs* (carnal self)." Sufis consider *jihad an-nafs*, struggle against the *nafs*, as a principle of life and discipline in God's path. It is considered the greater jihad. Part of the struggle implied humility, and the idea that a person was not better than anyone else.

"My mother might not be a scholar of Islam. However, when it comes to practice, she lived like a saint," said İbrahim. His mother would first apply what she taught to herself so that she could be a role model when teaching others. Naciye was a wise woman. İbrahim recalled his mother repeating the following: "If you educate a girl, you educate the whole family."

İbrahim noted, "My mother was like an advisor for my father. I have never witnessed my parents arguing with each other despite sometimes having different views. She would work to persuade him." The harmony in his parents' relationship showed İbrahim that much could be accomplished without resorting to conflict. Instead of arguing, İbrahim would use methods of persuasion, and if such methods did not work, he would remain silent. For İbrahim, this golden rule became a guiding principle.

MERAKLI KAHVE (CURIOUS COFFEE)

İbrahim's childhood was full of colorful moments, and he has not forgotten the events that have influenced his worldview. One such event was when İbrahim witnessed a Greek man making a special coffee for his father. The other event was the vision that he and his brother saw when they were playing in their back yard. It was a more profound, life-altering event.

First, let us discuss the "curious coffee" incident. When İbrahim's father walked along the street, everyone would greet him. Regardless of the language spoken individually, everyone knew the basics of each other's language. One day, when İbrahim was walking with his father along the main street of Larnaca, the Greek owner of a coffee shop greeted his father in Turkish and said he wanted to prepare a *"merakli kahve."* Although the Greek owner greeted İbrahim's father in Turkish, İbrahim did not understand what *merakli* meant but knew the meaning of *kahve* (coffee). He sat with his father and they drank the coffee that had been made by the Greek coffee shop owner.

İbrahim asked his father what *merakli kahve* meant. His father replied, "Son, this Greek is very respectful to our culture and to us. He knows that we do not start anything, including cooking, without saying *Bismillah*, in the name of God. Therefore, whenever he makes coffee for me, he says *Bismillah,* and then he calls this *merakli kahve* ("curious coffee," using the slang meaning of the word *merakli* to indicate respect). İbrahim then understood how respectful different ethnic groups could be to each other even when they prepare food.

MUTUAL RESPECT

In Cyprus at that time, it was very common for Muslims, Jews, Greeks, and Armenians to visit each other during their religious and cultural celebrations. This was an Ottoman custom. They would prepare homemade foods for each other's celebrations. When bringing food to İbrahim's house during special occasions, non-Muslim friends would take care to bring *halal* food. Similarly, when İbrahim's mother took food to non-Muslim friends, she would prepare the food based on their customs. İbrahim admired his parents' consideration for people of other faiths and ethnic groups. He continued their way of connecting with different people by caring for their needs.

Despite the animosity between Greece and Turkey at that time, his parents did not exhibit anti-Greek or anti-Armenian sentiments, so İbrahim would play with Armenian, Greek, and Jewish children without feeling superiority over them.

İbrahim stated, "The daughters of the Orthodox and Armenian priests would often visit my mum and, akin to the Muslim girls, they too would cover their hair. They would cook for us *bayram helva*, a special dessert for Eid[21]. Also, because I was still a child, they would bring a special gift for me. We never felt that they were different from

---

21   Major Islamic holiday occurring twice a year. The first is Eid al-Fitr, the first three days after the month of Ramadan when Muslims fast from dawn till sunset. The second is Eid al-Adha, four days during the Hajj, obligatory pilgrimage.

us. During their celebrations, my mother would cook foods that they enjoyed and take it with her when she visited them."

İbrahim added, "The things that I liked the most as a child were the serenity of our household, serving food to guests, and playing with children from other ethnic groups, regardless of what language they spoke or religion they followed."

For İbrahim, the house he lived in, the streets he wondered along, and the people he would spend his days with have left only pleasant traces in his mind. His house was not luxurious, but it was better shape than the houses nearby.

İbrahim lived in a two-story house that was surrounded by a wall in the upper class area of Larnaca. It had a spacious courtyard where the Dellals would often host guests. İbrahim's parents were very hospitable, cooking food every day in a *kazan* (cauldron) to distribute to any visitors, employees, or anyone in need. There were always two *kazan*s for the two dishes cooked daily. İbrahim recalled, "My mother took pleasure in cooking for those in need. Sometimes, the neighbors would come and help. Once the food was cooked, my mother would serve them as well. They would not turn anyone away from the food they cooked."

All guests were accepted as the "guests of God", and guests of God bring blessing and bounty to the house. In Turkish culture, the phrase "*tanrı misafiri*" or "God's guests" is common. The tradition of hospitality is rooted in Islam, which is an integral part of Turkish culture. Prophet Muhammad, peace be upon him, said, "Whoever believes in God and the Hereafter should serve his guest generously by giving him his reward"[22]. According to another saying of Prophet Muhammad, this hospitality has roots in the Abrahamic tradition as well. The Prophet Abraham would not sit for a meal that lacked guests. A meal with guests is called "Halil İbrahim Sofrasi" or "Abraham's Table." İbrahim reminisced, "When I was a child, I would serve the food to our guests with my father. My father would do this with

---

[22] Sahih Al-Bukhari, Volume 8, Number 48

such pleasure and honour. It was believed that serving guests would bring blessings to our family."

İbrahim's love for service had been implanted in him as a child. Serving others has been a custom since İbrahim's family first settled in Cyprus. This was a source of honour and pride for them and this culture of hospitality is a legacy of İbrahim's parents. İbrahim takes this as his inheritance, and it has become a central moral principle which guides his conduct.

For İbrahim, serving others is an act of worship. After his encounter with the Gülen Movement, İbrahim's love for giving to and working for others developed even further. Despite the fact that he retired in 1991, İbrahim keeps himself busy five, sometimes six, days a week with volunteer work. I asked him, "Isn't this difficult for you, especially at this age?" He looked at me in a matter-of-fact manner and replied, "If I don't do this, I will die. It is a part of my life, and I will do this until my last breath."

CHAPTER 3

The Hala Sultan Tekke, a Source of Inspiration

THE HALA SULTAN TEKKE,
A SOURCE OF INSPIRATION

Ibrahim would often visit Hala Sultan Tekke (Lodge), with his family when he was a child. The Lodge of Hala Sultan, also known as the Mosque of Umm Haram, is a prominent Muslim shrine located east of Saint Hilarion Castle, west of the Salt Lake, and southwest of the city of Larnaca. It is one of the revered sites in the Muslim world.

Umm Haram (or Hala Sultan in Turkish) was Prophet Muhammad's wet nurse and the wife of Ubada ibn as-Samid, a companion of the Prophet, peace be upon him.[23] She had followed the Prophet in his *hijra* (immigration) from Mecca to Medina in 622 A.D. Once during a short visit to Umm Haram's home, Prophet Muhammad shared with her a vision from God that Muslim believers would conquer the Mediterranean region and spread their faith. He also promised her that she would be among the first who would conquer an island, though it is not clear which island he referred to. Uthman ibn 'Affan the son-in-law, Companion of the Prophet, and third caliph[24] (644–656), launched a naval expedition against the Christian Byzantine people living in Cyprus in 649 A.D.

---

23 Nursi, Said, *Mektubat*, 1994, p. 105. Umm Haram came from the Banu Najjar tribe. This was the tribe of the Prophet Muhammad's great grandmother's tribe. Due to this connection, the Banu Najjar tribe and the Banu Hashim, the Prophet's tribe, held a strong connection, and referred to each other as aunt, uncle, or cousin even if no direct relation existed. This is why Umm Haram is called Hala Sultan in Turkish. Hala is the Turkish word for paternal aunt and Khala is the Arabic word for maternal aunt.

24 Caliph is the successor of Prophet Muhammad, peace be upon him, as the leader of the Muslim community

When the time came, Umm Haram joined her husband on board a battleship bound for Cyprus. Umm Haram remembered the vision that Prophet Muhammad, peace be upon him, had disclosed to her. She was eager to take part in this expedition to Cyprus and to be included as part of a formidable navy. The Arab navy with its powerful ships successfully defeated the Byzantine forces in Cyprus. According to some accounts, Umm Haram fell off her mule during the siege of Larnaca and died, possibly because of her advanced age. Her burial spot near Larnaca Salt Lake became a shrine and a mosque was built next to it during the early years of the 19th century.

Sheikh Hassan, a great Sufi, searched for Umm Haram's grave in 1760 and first erected the shrine structure. It was narrated that he saw a dream and then searched for the grave and successfully located it. Tradition holds that the great Sufi Sheik Hassan did not reveal to the general public the contents of the dream which led to his discovery of the grave site.

Later, a mosque was constructed on the site and the complex assumed its present form in 1817. The Lodge of Hala Sultan complex is composed of a mosque, mausoleum, minaret, cemetery, and living quarters for men and women. The term *tekke* (Sufi lodge) applies to a building designed specifically for the gatherings of a Sufi brotherhood, or *tariqah*, and may have referred to an earlier feature of the location like a cemetery of a saint. The present-day complex, open to all and not belonging to a single religious movement, lies in a serene setting on the shores of the Larnaca Salt Lake. Referred to as "the old woman's tomb", the Lodge is listed as a historical site by the Greek Cyprus government and is visited by Muslims, Christians, and tourists.

Within the mosque a wooden women's section and a wishing well can be found. The minaret is connected to the mosque at its northwestern corner. On the entrance gate there is an Ottoman inscription dated March 4, 1813. Sultan Mahmud II's monogram can be found on both sides of the inscription, which reads "The Lodge of Hala Sultan was built by God's beloved great Ottoman Cyprus governor." The garden was designed by a pasha (high ranking military officer), hence it is called the Pasha Garden. On the right side of the entrance there is a guesthouse for men (*selamlık*), while on the left side another guesthouse stands for women (*haramlık*)[25]. This tradition of separation of sexes existed in İbrahim's house and household, with separate guest rooms for men and women.

Visiting the Hala Sultan Lodge during religious holidays was a custom among Muslims living in Cyprus. The Dellal family would regularly visit the Lodge, especially during special religious events such as the Eids, Prophet Muhammad's birthday, and the Night of the Ascension of the Prophet to the Heavens[26]. They would usually visit the Lodge on the second day of Eid. The Dellal family would distribute food to fellow visitors. The imam of the mosque and other staff at Hala Sultan Lodge treated İbrahim's family with great respect. The family would stay the whole day and, on occasion, remain overnight.

Men and women worshiped in separate areas. The complex included a mosque and the land around the lodge belonged to the mosque. Income generated by the use of that land supported the lodge. İbrahim enjoyed playing in the fields surrounding the Lodge. Other children would also come to play there, especially during the days of Eid.

On Eid, children would kiss the hands of elders at the lodge. This is a common sign of respect in Turkish culture. The elders would give children sweets, money, and other small items. Even non-Muslim children would come to the lodge on the Eid days and kiss the hands of the elders, who would not hesitate in pleasing them with gifts as well.

A flower-like scent was always in the air when İbrahim visited this sacred place. İbrahim remarked, "There were flowers there, but

---

25 For more information, see Catia Galatariotou, *The Making of a Saint*, Cambridge University Press, 2004.

26 One of the important events of the Islamic calendar is Lailat al-Miraj, the Night of Ascension. On this night, it is believed that the Prophet ascended to the Heavens with the guidance of Archangel Gabriel. There, he met Adam, İbrahim (Abraham), Musa (Moses), and Isa (Jesus). Also, it was on this night that God ordained the five daily prayers for Muslims.

the smell was not like that of the flowers there or of any other flower for that matter." The scent remained a mystery for the young İbrahim who wondered if he was receiving the scent of Heaven's flowers through this revered place.

İbrahim loved the lodge so much that he would not be afraid to visit at night. A sense of calmness would descend upon him while he was there and he would look forward to his visits. İbrahim recalled, "I loved it more than I loved my house, as though some spiritual power would draw me there." The lodge was revered by Muslims and non-Muslims alike, there would be a mix of children for İbrahim to play with.

İBRAHİM'S MYSTICAL VISION

Although he can't remember the precise date, İbrahim assumes that he was younger than six years of age when he and his brother Hasan saw something truly amazing. One day, the two boys were playing in the backyard and both grew tired. İbrahim and Hasan lay side by side on the grass, staring up into the sky. Both boys saw the skies open up and saw a beautiful land with lush greenery. Then the boys saw themselves building a beautiful mosque. They were shocked but felt strangely happy.

İbrahim called for his mother, and said "Mum, come quickly!" When his mother came, İbrahim explained what they had witnessed, but when she looked up, she did not see anything in the sky. "You may have seen a dream," she responded. "No, mum. It wasn't a dream," said the brothers. "We weren't sleeping. How could we see a dream? Plus, both of us saw it." Naciye found it hard to believe. She shook her head and went into the house. The brothers later told their father what they had witnessed, but he too had a hard time believing it. For İbrahim, the vision was an unforgettable experience[27].

---

27 According to Islamic scholars, visions and dreams are not counted as religious knowledge. However, good dreams and visions can spiritually comfort a person and encourage that person to do more good. According to a hadith, "A true dream is one

This vision of İbrahim and Hasan came true many years later after they had settled in Australia. The brothers organized and directed the construction of the Cypriot Turkish Mosque in Sunshine, Victoria until its completion in 2001. "I later understood that God had shown my future of coming to Australia and building a mosque," he said.

Wishing to Be Poor

In 1938, İbrahim enrolled in primary school. Like many students, he cried a great deal during his first day at school; however, he eventually came to enjoy school. He liked his teacher and the teacher liked him as well. His father demonstrated a great deal of self-discipline, both at home and at work. Hence, he wanted İbrahim to study hard and also exhibit self-discipline. For example, İbrahim would go to school and return home on time.

During İbrahim's years at primary school, milk would be heated and distributed to the poor students. Because İbrahim was not poor, he did not receive. However, he greatly enjoyed the smell of the milk being heated. Even though his mother made milk at home, it never had the same smell. It was considered a disgrace to usurp the property of the poor or orphaned. Sometimes İbrahim wished he was poor so that he could have a taste of the milk. He was treated as a rich boy; however, he wanted to be treated as an ordinary boy.

İbrahim could not recall having committed naughty acts during his primary years. "Because of my family background, I could not do anything naughty at school. It would have been a disgrace for my family. Even if I did something wrong, I would be afraid of how my parents would react. Maybe I did some naughty things, but my teacher probably understood my situation and did not tell my parents," observed İbrahim.

---

part of the 66 parts of prophethood." In another hadith, Prophet Muhammad, peace be upon him, says, "Good dreams can be shared with close friends (if it is not for the purpose of showing off). Bad dreams should not be told to others." (Bukhari & Muslim) Scholars add that the more righteous a person is, the more truth there is in the dream. However, it is difficult to interpret dreams.

Teachers at the primary school provided religious lessons. In fact, İbrahim would have weekly religious lessons and the teachers would take Muslim students to the Friday congregational prayer session, which is akin to Sunday Mass in its significance.

During his primary school years, İbrahim was diagnosed with typhoid fever. At that time, typhoid fever was a serious, potentially fatal disease. Indeed, an abscess formed on İbrahim's hip and caused him great pain. The illness lasted several months. At first, his parents tried traditional cures. When nothing seemed to help, a physician was called in to examine the child. The physician removed the abscess. İbrahim recovered soon after. "When I think of it now, I thank God because I could have died from that," said İbrahim.

THE AMERICAN ACADEMY: A TURNING POINT

After the British gained control over Cyprus in 1878, Ottoman-style education on the island weakened, especially after the annexation in 1917. The British abolished the *awqaf* educational system where Cypriot Turkish teachers received their salaries. There were no decent Turkish high schools in Larnaca due to lack of funds, so Hasan Hüseyin Effendi sent his older son, Hasan, and then İbrahim, to the American Academy, which had a good academic reputation. While it would have been very odd for a mufti's son to send his children to a Christian missionary school, he did not have other options. The American Academy offered an excellent education. The school was expensive; however, İbrahim's father wanted his children to have the best possible education.

During the last quarter of the 19th century and the beginning of 20th century, missionaries had opened a number of schools through-out the Ottoman Empire including Cyprus. The Foreign Mission Board of the Reformed Presbyterian Church of North America founded the American Academy in Larnaca in 1908.

Staff members of the school tried to instill "the Academy spirit" in each student. Staff members encouraged students to show respect for each other and promoted understanding and co-operation between students and staff. Moreover, the school encouraged student and staff involvement in humanitarian, social, cultural, and other activities designed to benefit the greater community.

İbrahim was further exposed to different cultural traditions since both students and faculty members were drawn from various ethnic enclaves including Cypriot Turkish, Cypriot Greek, Maronite, and Armenian. In addition, foreign nationals attended the school.

At the academy, all lectures were delivered in English and students were not allowed to use non-English languages. If a student was caught conversing in Turkish, Greek, or other non-English languages on school grounds, his/her grade would be reduced.

The administrators and some of the teachers were evangelical Protestants, but were dedicated to education first. Furthermore, they would tend to all of their students' varying needs and problems and worked to raise the students to be disciplined, cultured, and well mannered.

Before lessons started at 9am, it was obligatory for students to attend a prayer session in the school chapel. However, those who did not wish to say their prayers while at the chapel were not obliged to do so, such as İbrahim and some other students. Despite some students complaining to their parents about the morning prayer service, no action was taken by administrators.

İbrahim was successful in the school and Ms. Fuller was his favorite teacher. She was quite religious. Moreover, she was a kind, disciplined, and effective instructor. She would often give advice to İbrahim.

Some of the things İbrahim learned at school contradicted what he had learned at home. His instructors taught Ottoman history differently to what İbrahim learned from his family. İbrahim envisioned the Ottomans as civilized people, dedicated to justice and social welfare, whereas his history books would depict an imperialist empire expanded by the sword. Doubts were forming in his mind about the grand empire his family was loyal to. He was hesitant to voice his doubts to his parents out of fear that they would withdraw him from school.

There were more issues that added to the clash of cultures. Despite enjoying the dance lessons at school, İbrahim did not continue attending these lessons due to his religious and cultural background which enforced separation of the sexes. He was wary of what his parents would say if they found out about the few dancing lessons he took. During the 1940s, Larnaca was still conservative in terms of family values and relations. Boys and girls would mingle at school, but mixed activities would not occur too often after school.

İbrahim questioned which way was correct: the lifestyle he experienced in school or at home. This uncertainty distracted İbrahim from his studies from time to time. Sometimes he was left under greater impression by his school life but as he pondered over it, he felt guilty. Most of the time, he wanted to follow his parents' teachings instead of the school's teachings. There were some students who converted to Protestantism from Greek Orthodoxy, Armenian Orthodoxy and Judaism. İbrahim added, "There were a few Turks, but I had not known of any of them to change their faiths at the Academy."

Despite the differences in the lifestyles İbrahim experienced, he generally enjoyed his years in high school. He was a popular student. İbrahim would always dress well, and being a handsome boy, would be admired by the girls, though he would hesitate to mingle with them. He was from a relatively wealthy family, disciplined, good at his schoolwork, excelled in athletics, and had good manners.

Just as how İbrahim did not forget the milk served to the poor students in his primary school, he did not forget the olive pastries served during breakfast at the Academy. This was İbrahim's favorite food at school. He remarked, "Because it was made wholly of natural ingredients, it had a very sweet scent, unlike olive pastries prepared with artificial ingredients."

There was one bad experience at the Academy that İbrahim did not forget. Someone had broken a window of the school. İbrahim was there at the time; however, he did not cause the damage. One of the Greek teachers accused İbrahim of the misdeed. İbrahim was unable to convince the teacher otherwise. İbrahim was punished and his father had to pay for the damage. İbrahim felt very demoralized since he attached great importance to his honor. Indeed, İbrahim felt that some of the Greek teachers treated him unfairly.

İbrahim found history to be a particularly intriguing topic, and despite some of the different views presented, he liked his history lessons. He grew up hearing stories of his family, the Ottoman Empire, and significant Muslims, like the prophets, companions, and saints. He would read history books in the school's library. "If I pursued further education, I would aspire to become a professor of history," İbrahim said. During my interviews with İbrahim I learned that his passion for the study of history has remained strong and he continues to review books, speeches, and documentaries.

While still in high school, he began attending the British Institute of Technology in Larnaca. During the day, he went to the American Academy, while at nights and on weekends he would attend the British Institute of Technology where he completed an automotive engineering course. İbrahim was an average student; however, he excelled in sports.

Following the defeat of Nazi Germany, there was a celebration in Larnaca. İbrahim attended the celebration. When he returned home after his curfew of 7 pm, he saw his father's cross face. Indeed, his father was so disappointed and angry that he slapped İbrahim's face. İbrahim observed that this was the first and last time that his father would employ corporal punishment. İbrahim did not retaliate in anger. Nevertheless, he was shocked and saddened. İbrahim was also upset that he had violated one of his father's rules. "I have only seen compassion from my parents. This was the one time, I had been punished like this," recalled İbrahim.

CHAPTER 4

Immigration to Australia

IMMIGRATION TO AUSTRALIA

When Cyprus was under the control of the United Kingdom, all citizens could apply for an English passport. In 1948, İbrahim's older brothers, Hasan and Ahmet, left Cyprus due to the rising political and ethnic tensions between the Turks and the Greeks. They settled in the state of Victoria in Australia. İbrahim would frequently write to them. The letters he received in return led İbrahim to consider moving to Australia. As his excitement grew, İbrahim finally decided to settle in Australia in 1950. However, his parents were opposed to the idea. Moreover, his parents wanted İbrahim to remain in Cyprus and manage the family business.

When İbrahim revealed his plans to his parents, they tried to persuade him to remain in Cyprus. İbrahim postponed his travel plans. He did not wish to upset his parents; however, his desire to travel to Australia continued to grow. He continued to wrestle with the problem and finally told his parents that he would remain in Australia for a few years only, and then return to Cyprus. Upon hearing this, his parents did not say anything. Culturally, silence in this situation indicates consent that is undesirable, a subtle way of saying, "Do as you wish."

İbrahim was granted a permit to enter Australia. On the permit, he was not classified as a Cypriot Turk, but rather as a "British Subject by Birth." For his religion, it is written "Not Jewish but Mohammedan," presumably because the term "Muslim" was not well known at that time, which is ironic considering the long history of Muslims in Australia and the work of the Afghan camel-drivers with Australian pioneers in exploring and mapping the country.

After applying for permanent residency, İbrahim planned on sailing from Cyprus to Alexandria, Egypt. He would stay in Egypt for a night and then board another ship bound for Australia. The day had finally come for him to go. His parents took him to Laymosun Port, but it was very hard for İbrahim and his parents to part. All three were crying when İbrahim boarded the ship. As the ship departed İbrahim continued to wave to his parents until they were out of sight. At the age of 18, İbrahim was off to the other side of the world.

The ship stopped in Alexandria, Egypt, where İbrahim stayed at a hotel. In the evening, the hotel owner called İbrahim. The hotel owner told İbrahim that he had visitors waiting for him downstairs. İbrahim was surprised since he did not know anyone in Egypt. He went downstairs and met a man surrounded by security personnel. The man said that he was Suleiman, the nephew of King Farouk of Egypt. "Your father is a friend of ours," said Suleiman.

Apparently, İbrahim's father sent a telegram to Suleiman after İbrahim left. He urged Suleiman to persuade İbrahim to return home. Suleiman and İbrahim went up to İbrahim's room and talked for more than an hour. Suleiman tried to convince İbrahim to return to Cyprus or even stay in Egypt; however, Suleiman was not successful.

Before Suleiman left the hotel, he gave İbrahim a blank signed check and said that İbrahim was free to withdraw as much money as he wanted from Suleiman's account. İbrahim thanked him for this and the following morning left for Australia. İbrahim never cashed the check. Indeed, he treasured this check for approximately thirty years until he lost it when he moved into a new house.

İbrahim stated that his real struggle to serve others started on the ship, *Ocean Triumph*, bound for Australia. Since he grew up watching his parents helping others and he had always been encouraged to do so himself, he would try hard to help others. He met with four anxious men, two Greek and two Turkish, who could not speak English, hence could not communicate with the crew. Since İbrahim had learned Greek as a child in Cyprus, he translated for the four men on board the *Ocean Triumph*.

The journey took roughly six weeks. During the voyage, İbrahim doubted whether he had made the right decision by leaving his parents. He cried several times. After six weeks, the *Ocean Triumph* arrived in

Melbourne at approximately 5 am on 28 April, 1950, at Victoria Dock. İbrahim could not leave the ship until 9 pm as there were other ships that were loading and unloading their cargo on the busy dock.

Before going to his brother's house, İbrahim helped his Greek friends. He hailed a taxi and took the Greeks to one of their relatives who owned a fish shop in Brunswick. They had a light meal together and spoke with each other. He then took one of the Turks to a restaurant, where he spent some time in conversation. He took the second Turk to Rosewater. One of these two Turks who journeyed with İbrahim is still alive, but due to his physical condition is unable to talk much.

It was close to midnight when İbrahim arrived at his brother Ahmet's house. The lights were still on. When he knocked on the door, Ahmet opened the door. He was very surprised since no one told him when İbrahim would be coming. They conversed until 4 am. Since İbrahim's brother had to go to work at 8 am, they were forced to end their conversation and went to sleep.

In a recently published book of memoirs, *Yesterday and Today: Turkish Cypriots of Australia*, İbrahim stated, "In the years we came from Cyprus to Australia, I am guessing the population of Australia was about 6.5 to 7 million. Of course, since, during those times, they were *'önculer'* (pioneers) since there were few people coming from Cyprus. Those who came did not know English. Those who knew English were numbered. I guess there were about 150–200 Cyprus Turks.[28]" (PICTURE 2)

EARLY YEARS IN AUSTRALIA

The first few months in Australia were very difficult for İbrahim, but he had an advantage that many other immigrants did not: he knew how to speak and write in English due to his education at the American Academy. He obtained an entry-level position as an automotive

---

[28] Serkan Hussein & Edward Carusu, *Yesterday & Today: Turkish Cypriots of Australia.* PromozPlus, Melbourne. 2007.

engineer in an engineering plant in Essendon, Victoria. He lived with his older brother, Ahmet, in Reservoir. The trip from his brother's home to the plant in Essendon was arduous, taking three hours one way, and including a half-hour walk and two trains. There were few trains and buses available for communities in the 1950s.

After spending five or six months in Australia, İbrahim became homesick. Not only were there few Turks and Muslims, but there was also less acceptance of immigrants. İbrahim said, "If my brother and I spoke Turkish in the presence of an Australian, he or she would tell us to speak in English. Our difference was not accepted like it is today." All of this added to İbrahim's longing to go home. He recalled, "Those years were very lonely."

During the 1950s, the mail service was the only means of communication between Australia and Cyprus; therefore İbrahim frequently sent letters to his parents. Even if he wanted to visit his parents, flights from Australia to Cyprus were rare and unaffordable. A return trip to Cyprus by ship would have been inconvenient since it took a minimum of three months. Therefore, İbrahim decided to return to Cyprus after several years.

A few months after arriving in Australia, he landed a new job at the post office located in South Melbourne. He quit his first job, thus avoiding the long commute of his previous job. He liked the peace that his new job brought. It was a cleaner work setting since he was no longer working on cars. It was closer to his home. Also, it was a tranquil work environment.

During his first week, his coworkers approached him, saying "It's tradition for the new worker to come with us to the trough." İbrahim was confused. He knew a trough was where farm animals drank water. He said, "Because I did not want to be impolite, I did not ask them what they meant, thinking they may have meant something else."

On the first Friday, İbrahim left work a bit early with the other workers to go to "the trough." They walked to the pub on the corner of Flinders and Swanston Street, which still stands today. At the bar, the others ordered drinks, and told İbrahim to drink up. İbrahim stated that he couldn't. İbrahim remembered the look on their face. He said, "They were surprised at seeing a man in Australia who would not drink." Fortunately, the bar attendant understood and offered İbrahim a lemonade. Not too long after, he said, "Thank you so much, boys. I have to go," and slipped out. İbrahim also added one aspect about Australia's past that he missed. He mentioned, "In the 1950s, pubs used to close at 6 pm. After 6 pm, people would just take their purchased cans of beer and drink outside. That's what my friends did after I left, according to what they told me on Monday."

Through this experience, İbrahim came to understand the place of alcohol in Australian culture. He saw that his coworkers and friends would drink after work, especially on Fridays, as a tradition, and on weekend gatherings. Despite the prevalent culture and peer pressure, İbrahim stood by his religious principle of not drinking alcohol. Yet, not wanting to accept this tradition, he felt lonely. It was experiences like these which made İbrahim feel far away from home.

İBRAHİM'S FIRST ANZAC DAY

Along with the drinking traditions, İbrahim was not aware of many culturally and historically significant days. It was through his coworkers that he learned what mattered to Australians.

At the post office, İbrahim was a respected worker. During his first year, he was guided and helped by a man named Lenny in both work-related and personal issues.

> It was March of 1951 when Lenny and I were having lunch in the cafeteria. A man named Terry approached me and said, "You killed my uncle." I was dumbfounded. I had no idea what he was referring to. Lenny told me to ignore him and not reply. When he left, Lenny told me that Terry's uncle died in Gallipoli. My knowledge of Gallipoli's history and its place in Australia's history was little. The next day, Terry came at lunch and said the same things again. Lenny stepped on my foot to remind me not to respond.
>
> The third day, Terry came again and accused me. I stood up and said, "That's enough. Tell me. Did your uncle go to Gallipoli with

uniform or without uniform? Did your uncle go to Gallipoli with arms or without arms?" He replied, "Of course! With uniform and arms." I replied, "Well then, what do you expect? Do you think we should have greeted him with flowers? Our people had no business with them. They went there to kill us, and they got killed. My uncle died there too." Terry did not reply. Lenny came to my side and said, "That was a battle. Those who take part in a battle kill and get killed. Let's not talk about this again." Terry never brought up the subject again.

Anzac Day is a national day of remembrance and public holiday to honour members of the Australian and New Zealand Army Corps (ANZAC) at Gallipoli in Turkey during World War I. Observed since 1916, Anzac Day is one of the most solemn days in Australia, dedicated not only to the soldiers who fought at Gallipoli, but to all armed forces in past wars.

POOR LITTLE JOHN

One of İbrahim's coworkers, who was called "Little John" due to his height and he had a drinking problem. He would drink every day after work, and consume beer during work as well, although not enough to appear drunk. Most of the times, his coworkers would have to escort him home because he was too drunk to take care of himself. One day, İbrahim's coworkers asked İbrahim for a favor. "Can you take Little John home today?" Not being one to turn down someone in need, İbrahim agreed.

After Little John had some drinks, İbrahim escorted him to his home in North Richmond by train. Little John couldn't walk straight and fell behind. In his drunk condition, he managed to direct İbrahim to his house. İbrahim remembers what happened when they arrive at the house:

> We arrived at the door, and I rang the bell. Little John was standing behind me. I turned to him, and the next thing I knew, a huge arm went past my face and grabbed Little John. He was pulled inside the house, and I had barely seconds to see the huge woman slam the door on my face. She started yelling at him, saying, "You

drank again, didn't you?" Then I heard all this noise. It sounded like she was beating poor Little John up. I went home. I was in shock for about a week from seeing the woman's arm whisk Little John away suddenly. Later, I learned that the coworkers would escort Little John home so that his wife would not hurt him.

In 1960, he reached the position of postmaster general. Years later, İbrahim further demonstrated his management skills working as a supervisor at an electric company owned by Telecom Australia. He was in charge of the city's generators, maintained in case of a blackout. He supervised 75 employees. İbrahim felt the weight of the position on his shoulders, and kept alert in case the generators would need to be put into use. His sense of responsibility made him a reliable supervisor.

The Golden Fifties

As a young and handsome man, İbrahim would be approached by women during his commute to and from work. Of course, he was a modest man and did not respond. He recalled:

> Back then, the trains wouldn't come as often. During the morning and afternoon commute, it was possible to see the same faces. There were these two girls, one light-skinned blonde and one tanned brunette. They would flirt with me and try to get me to talk, but I would hesitate because of the way my parents raised me. I would get embarrassed by such things. Sometimes, they would make rude remarks when I would not respond to their advances, saying things like, "What kind of a man is he?" I would even change compartments at train stops just to save myself from them.
>
> Sadly, we had to be in the same bus every day. One day, they got off at the same stop which was near my brother's house where I was living at the time. All the way home, they kept yelling things at me like, "Aren't you a man? Aren't we girls? Are we ugly? Why don't you talk to us? Why don't you look at us?" My brother's wife, Iclal, was at the door, hearing all these. I was embarrassed that she saw this.

İbrahim's reaction was not unusual considering the social culture of the fifties when dating was still not as acceptable as it is today. Public gestures of love were rare and looked down upon. İbrahim was raised to respect women, and that meant conversing with them in a serious and polite manner. He understood there to be a limit between men and women in conversation. İbrahim recalled:

> There's even a stranger story. There was a beautiful Catholic girl in my neighbourhood who attached herself to me. A few times, she followed me and tried to strike a conversation with me. She too made similar remarks that the two girls on the train would make to me. I did not respond to her advances either. Years later, I was attending a friends' funeral at a Catholic church. That Catholic girl was there, but as a nun! She came up to me and said, "İbrahim, you're still as handsome as you used to be." I had no idea how to reply to that. I just smiled.

Despite the aforementioned incidents, İbrahim misses living in the fifties in Australia. He recalled, "In the fifties, if my car broke down on the side of a street, someone would eventually pull over and help. At work, all my coworkers, including Terry, were honest and trustworthy people. We enjoyed friendship, mateship[29], and fellowship. We were like a family."

İbrahim reminisced, "The crime rates were low too. We would not lock our doors. On the days milk was delivered, we would leave money in the mailbox for the milkman and he would leave the milk. He would leave the change behind as well. Neither our money or milk was ever taken."

İbrahim believes that community relations were stronger during the 1950s. Neighbours would visit and take care of each other in times of need. Friends would trust each other more, and live less isolated lives. İbrahim referred to Professor Fred Hollows' statement "Sex, alcohol, and secular goodness surgically removed my Christianity, leaving no scars."[30] İbrahim added "He was right. Secularism took

---

[29] In Australian slang, "mate" is used to refer to a good friend.
[30] *The Age* (Australian Daily Newspaper), 30 January 1993.

away many values not just from Christians, but everyone, including Muslims."

Banjo Club

In the 1950s, the tango and Welsh music were popular. He joined the Victoria Banjo Club, a musical group at the time[31]. İbrahim was not unfamiliar with Western music. While he was a student at the American Academy, he became familiar with Western music and instruments. İbrahim also played the organ and piano. His friends admired him for his talent. The Victoria Banjo Club gave a concert at the Melbourne Town Hall and Treasure Garden. On one occasion, after giving a concert in Treasure Garden, a few Australian girls came up to him and started to speak enthusiastically with him. There were a few young Australian men who were not happy with this develop-ment due to jealousy. They tried to intimidate him and intended to beat him up. The girls nearby stopped any fight from occurring. This did not sit well with İbrahim. He did not like being the centre of con-flict since he was a bridge-builder by nature, nor did he like the way he was treated by the girls. He thought for days and finally decided to quit the Banjo Club in 1952.

Looking for Olive Oil

One cause of homesickness was the lack of accustomed food. People generally miss the cooking of their parents, particularly their mothers. İbrahim missed his mother's beans, stuffed peppers, bulgur (cracked wheat rice), and grape leaves marinated with olive oil. Even though İbrahim had moved out of his brother's house to the house next door,

---

[31] The Victoria Banjo Club was originally formed in 1932 by Charles Bowden and was later run by his son Ian. During the height of its popularity from the 1930s to the late 1950s, the Club had a headquarters and music store in central Melbourne and boasted a membership numbering in the hundreds. It's motto was "to create music is the greatest thrill". The Victoria Banjo Club was originally named Melbourne Banjo Club, which was established in the 1920's by Conan E. ('Bill') Andrews.(http://www.victoriabanjoclub.com.au/about.html)

he would visit Ahmet's home to eat his wife's home-cooked Turkish meals. However, it was never the same as his mother's meals. His brothers could not find the necessary Turkish ingredients.

Olive oil is an essential ingredient in many Mediterranean dishes. Islamically, olive oil is considered to have medicinal properties.[32] İbrahim loved to eat salad with olive oil. Unfortunately, he could not find olive oil in the markets during his early years in Australia. He said:

> In the first few years that I was in Australia, I missed olive oil a lot, especially in salads. I could not find it in the markets. There was only animal fat available for use as an oil-like ingredient. One day, a friend told me to go to the pharmacy where olive oil was sold as a medicinal item. When I went to the pharmacy and asked for olive oil, the pharmacist brought me a small 10mL bottle. I bought two, came home, and mixed some into my salad. I had missed it so much that I finished the two bottles in two days in salads.
>
> I went to the pharmacist again and asked him for eight more bottles. He was surprised and asked, 'Didn't you get two bottles just a few days ago? What do you do with all that olive oil to finish it so quickly?' I replied, 'In my country, we use it when cooking food or in salads.' The pharmacist was surprised, and brought eight more bottles. I was so happy that I found olive oil.

Sometime after 1957, a Greek businessman opened a shop called the "Violinist" on Lonsdale Street in the city of Melbourne. The Greek businessman sold imported Greek foods and ingredients. Since Turkish and Greek cuisine have a great deal in common, İbrahim and other Turks would shop at the Violinist. "That Greek man earned quite a deal of money since he was the only one in all of Melbourne who offered the foods and products we needed," added İbrahim.

İbrahim recalled, "After we started buying from that store, our Australian neighbours who would see our ingredients, such as lentils, chick peas, and bulgur (cracked wheat), and would wonder what

---

32 Prophet Muhammad, peace be upon him, said, "Eat olive oil and anoint yourselves with it, for it comes from a blessed tree. (Narrated by Tirmidhi and Ibn Maja)

these strange things were. Back then, the main foods were fish and chips, pie, pastry, and meat dishes."

I heard a similar story during an interview with another Cypriot Turk, Mehmet Salih, who emigrated after the Second World War. Mehmet loved yogurt, but could not find it in Australia. His Greek friend returned from his trip to Cyprus with some yogurt. He gave Mehmet a small amount to use as starter culture to make yogurt. Mehmet's wife made yogurt and packed it for her husband's lunch.

During lunch hour at the factory, Mehmet's Australian coworkers were curious about the cream-like food Mehmet was eating. The supervisor joined the conversation about this strange food and grew suspicious after smelling the yogurt. He then called the manager, who examined the yogurt and insisted that Mehmet was trying to consume expired milk so that he would become sick and receive compensation. He immediately threw the yogurt away. "Now, the funny thing is, Australians eat more yogurt than I do," joked Mehmet. When I told İbrahim this story, he nodded and said, "That's true. There was no yogurt then either."

THE MOHAMMADAN CHAPEL

During the first few years that İbrahim lived in Australia, he felt that he was living in a spiritual desert. The spiritual atmosphere in his parents' home had nourished his soul, but he was deprived of this spiritual sustenance in Australia. He sought to obtain that nourishment in Australia by spending time with good Muslims and attending Friday prayer sessions.

Bilal Cleland, author of *The Muslims in Australia: A Brief History*, writes that until 1957 there were no established mosques in Victoria, Muslims residing in Melbourne and surrounding areas would organize congregational prayers in their homes[33]. However, Cleland's book fails to mention the Mohammedan Chapel.

---

[33] Bilal Cleeland, The Muslims in Australia: A Brief History, 2002, Islamic Council of Victoria, Melbourne, p.77.

It was in either 1951 or 1952 that a grandson of one of the Afghan camel drivers[34] took İbrahim for Eid Prayer to the Mohammadan Chapel in Fawkner Memorial Park. İbrahim cannot recall who lead the prayer, but thinks that it may have been a Bosnian or Albanian layperson. İbrahim and I went to see the Chapel. The Mohammadan Chapel is a small, one room brick building. Covered with a basic roof, the Chapel received light through two windows. There is nothing in the room that reflects the art or furniture found in established mosques. It was a simple prayer room. While the building still stands, it is currently used as a storage area and prayer sessions are no longer held in the building. The *qiblah*[35] is not accurate, but not far off from the right direction. (PICTURE 3)

The original wooden doors and sign remain, although the sign has been painted over and now reads "Islamic Society of Victoria." The worn sign begins with the Arabic "Bismillahir Rahmanir Rahim," meaning, "In the Name of God, Most Compassionate, Most Merciful," which begins almost every chapter in the Qur'an. Below that are four verses in Arabic. "*O soul, that are at rest! Return to your Lord, well-pleased (with him), well-pleasing (Him). So enter among My servants. And enter into My garden*" (89:27-30). Underneath that, the English words "Islamic Cemetery" remain clearer than the verses in its green lettering.

İbrahim noted that the land where the chapel sits was first purchased by Muslims with the intention of building a mosque, but financial limitations allowed them to construct only a small prayer area. The outlying land began to be used as burial grounds. Graves reflect the history of Muslims in Australia including the Afghan camel drivers who passed away during the 1940s, Albanian immigrants who came after the Second World War, Cypriots Turks who immigrated to Australia, and Turks who were once under British rule. The last

---

34 Afghan camel drivers played a significant role in mapping the Australian terrain during the early days of settlement. They were brought over by British settlers.

35 Muslims pray five times a day towards the Ka'bah, the holiest mosque located in Mecca, Saudi Arabia. It is a requirement of prayer to face towards Ka'bah, which is called the Qiblah.

burial occurred in 1972. Due to neglect, it is uncertain where some graves are located or who lies beneath the gravestones.

The name "Mohammedan Chapel" is a rather odd choice since Christians primarily use the term "chapel," and Muslims do not use the term "Mohammedan." İbrahim explained, "It seems that the locals who were not informed about the Islamic faith called the building a chapel. Possibly, the original builders did not protest against the term, not knowing the implications. But it has been painted over."

The term "Mohammedan" is an archaic term once used by Westerners to describe Muslims. Since the term Christianity was used to describe the religion founded by Jesus Christ, Western traders and travelers to Muslim lands named Islam after its holiest figure, Prophet Muhammad, not knowing how inaccurate that label is since Muslims do not see Muhammad as a deity. This archaic term had been used until the mid-1960s, but is not welcomed among Muslims.[36]

İbrahim explained that during the 1950s Muslims living in Australia had a difficult time determining when Ramadan and other Islamic holy days would occur since Muslim emigrants had relied on mosques in their countries of origin.

During his first years in Australia, İbrahim was unable to attend Friday prayer because there was no mosque nearby, and he did not know other Muslims living nearby to form a congregation. However, he would find ways to attend Eid prayers. When he finally met the grandchildren of an Afghan camel-driver, he was able to attend Friday prayer at the newly established Mohammedan Chapel on several occasions. At that time, there were fewer than a dozen Muslims attending the prayer sessions. Sometimes, he was not able to leave work and attend prayer.

In the mid 1950s, İbrahim met Imam Fehmi. İbrahim's relationship with the Imam was a crucial event in his spiritual journey. Now, he had someone to help him explore religious matters. In return, he

---

[36] Montgomery Watt, *Muhammad: Prophet and Statesman.* Oxford University Press, London, 1961, p. 229.

would help Imam Fehmi improve his English since the Imam was not a fluent speaker of English. İbrahim made use of the advancement of radio technology after the 1960s and used short-wave radio to tune into Turkish news. He was finally able to determine the timing of Ramadan and the dates of holy days.

ENCOUNTERING EARLY MUSLIMS

İbrahim received a phone call from the University of Melbourne regarding a translation of an Ottoman script to English. He was unsure of how they found his contact information. İbrahim did not know the Ottoman script; however, he offered to look for someone who did.

After some time, İbrahim was told by an acquaintance that there was a man called Hüseyin Ara Efendi who immigrated from Istanbul at the end of the 19th century to Geelong, 75km south-west of Melbourne. Believing that this man could read Ottoman script, İbrahim went to Geelong to meet him. Upon arriving to Geelong, İbrahim saw that Hüseyin was old and blind, hence unable to translate any text.

İbrahim was curious about this Ottoman Turk. He learned that, despite his blindness, Hüseyin would have a family member take him to the seashore where he would fish. Later in the day, the fish that he caught would be sold in the market. This way, he was able to earn some money for his family. He did not accept money from anyone, including welfare agencies, because in Ottoman culture, it was a shame to rely on someone else. Hüseyin Ara Efendi wanted to uphold his dignity. Afterwards, İbrahim did not hear of Hüseyin, but heard that his children were still there. Hüseyin's sense of indebtedness and self-reliance reminded İbrahim of his parents, evoking a feeling of homesickness, and left a permanent mark in his memories.

Hüseyin Ara Efendi was one of the early Muslims İbrahim encountered during the 1950s. İbrahim also met with Ali Acem Efendi, a former camel driver who became a businessman and a prominent doctor, and Ali Baba, another former camel-driver, in his brother Ahmet's house. Ali Acem Efendi lived in Adelaide, and would visit the Dellals when he had business in Melbourne. Ali Acem shared his memories of his days as a camel driver. However, İbrahim did not document these stories.

Ali Acem was also an herbalist. İbrahim's sister-in-law, Iclal, had a problem with her hands. They would bleed after washing dishes. Local physicians were unable to help her; however, Ali Acem produced a medicine using herbs. After using the herbal medication for some time, Iclal's hands healed. Ali Acem had permission from the Australian government to use such herbs. Indeed, famous individuals would also use his products for various ailments.

Ali Acem and Ali Baba shared their immigration stories with the Dellals. They arrived in Australia with four other friends (four have since passed away). Ali Acem took Ali Baba to Broken Hill, NSW, where there was a small mosque and grandchildren of the earlier Afghan camel drivers. Ali Baba decided to live in Broken Hill since he conducted business there. When Ali Baba became dependant, Ali Acem hired an Aboriginal man to take care of Ali Baba. When Ali Baba passed away, he was buried at Broken Hill.

Ali Acem was well off financially. He owned a truck and transported automotive parts around major cities. When he passed away, there was no one to check in on him since his wife had died years earlier and his two daughters had left home years ago and cut off relations with him. The police who found Ali Acem's corpse took out a piece of paper from his pocket. It was Ahmet Dellal's business card. They contacted Ahmet, but since Ahmet did not know any of Ali Acem's relatives, the police arranged for Ali Acem's burial. This disturbed İbrahim. "It was very bitter that one of our own died alone, and that his daughters had nothing to do with him."

İbrahim was fortunate to meet not just one, but several cameldrivers who contributed to the exploration of and transportation across the Australian outback. İbrahim regretted that he could not remember most of their stories. He said, "I wish I had written their stories. They were so fascinating."

Seven Year Trip to Australia

One of the few Muslim families that the Dellals were close to in the 1950s was the Aceyoğlu family. İbrahim and Mehmet Aceyoğlu were good friends and worked closely together in Muslim community activities and were good friends until Mehmet's death in 1978. Mehmet's experiences and views left a deep impression on İbrahim, who took Mehmet as a sort of mentor in community service despite some cultural differences. It is not possible to focus only on Mehmet's life after arriving in Australia when his past gave him different perspectives on Australian people and lifestyle. The Aceyoğlu's seven-year journey alone could be the focus of a biography. The family's saga illustrates the tragedy and hardships immigrants faced before and after settling in Australia.

İbrahim and I visited Mehmet's widow, Asiye, several times to hear the family's story firsthand. İbrahim had arranged my interview session with her. A healthy 91-year-old woman, Asiye lives with her son in the city of Melbourne. At first, she was hesitant to reveal her past since it was full of pain and sadness. "If I start to tell you, I could go on for days," she remarked. İbrahim explained the significance of recording memories for future generations. He emphasized that documenting such memories would help to keep her deceased husband's memory alive. This stirred her feelings, and she slowly opened up. She took out some photos and objects that were reminders of her family's past.

The Aceyoğlu family originally lived in Karachai, which was populated by the Muslim Turkic people of North Caucasus. Karachai is located on the border of Russia near Georgia.

World War II lead to the displacement of millions of people. The Aceyoğlu family left their country, and travelled to Europe in search for a better life. In 1947, the family used connections to board a train to Naples, Italy. They applied to different consulates, including the Turkish consulate, for permission to emigrate, but they did not receive permission, "Naples was full of war refugees then. There were no jobs, and the crime rate was high," Mehmet's wife reported. When passing by the docks, the Aceyoğlu brothers noticed a ship with a crescent flag, commonly used by Muslims. They approach the sailors and enquired further, and learned that the ship belonged to an Egyptian Prince named Amir İbrahim, whose wife was the granddaughter of an Ottoman Sultan.

It was not long before the brothers met with the Egyptian Prince and his Turkish wife, a relative of the last Ottoman sultan. They told their story of loss and difficulty. Wanting to help the family, Prince Amir İbrahim sent a telegram to Egypt to get permanent residency for the Aceyoğlus and some other Turkic Muslims. Within one day, the return telegram gave the fortunate news of residency in Egypt. Together with the Prince, the Aceyoğlu family and the other Turkic Muslims traveled to Egypt. During the journey, the Ottoman princess spent time with the Aceyoğlus.

When the ship arrived in Alexandria, Egypt, the prince did not allow the newcomers to enter the city since there was an outbreak of cholera. Therefore, the newcomers stayed in a quarantined camp for four weeks until the city was secure. Then the prince took the family to his guesthouse. Asiye was grateful to the Prince. She said, "He took good care of us. The house was beautiful, and had a big garden. He placed three servants to help us: one to clean the house and do the laundry, one to do the shopping, and one to take care of the children. I did not want to accept servants because I am not used to being served. It wasn't until I got many stares as a white woman among the darker-skinned Egyptians while shopping that I accepted one servant to do the shopping."

"We stayed there for about two years, and for two years, the prince took care of us. He sent over a sewing machine for me when I told him that I could sew and use my time productively. Even though it is old, I still keep that machine to remember his kindness. I also have the meat grinder he sent." As a token of their appreciation and love towards the prince and princess, the Aceyoğlu family named their newborn daughter "Farida" after Egyptian Queen Farida.

During this period, Mehmet and İbrahim continued to search for immigration opportunities. "The prince told my husband that socialists were gaining strength in Egypt, so his power and protection was not guaranteed. He suggested we go elsewhere. He promised to support us wherever we chose to go by covering travel expenses," said Asiye. Mehmet went to the Turkish consulate many times to determine the status of his application until consulate officials literally threw him out for his persistence. On the ground, Mehmet swore to the officials, "I will never step foot on Turkish soil!"

When Mehmet heard that the Australian government was accepting immigrants, he went to the Australian high commissioner in Cairo to apply. The Aceyoğlu family was called in for an interview with the high commissioner, and they told their story of escape from Russia. They were called again after a few days. The commissioner's first words upon seeing them were, "Welcome to Australia." He shook Mehmet's hand and said, "Australia needs hardworking people like you." The necessary forms were filled out, and travel expenses were covered by the prince. The family expressed their gratitude to the prince and princess. (Picture 4)

A day before leaving for Australia, an official from the Turkish consulate came to see Mehmet. The consulate had accepted his application for residency in Turkey. Mehmet replied, "I have been at your door for two years. You threw me out too. I swore that I would not step foot in Turkey, so I reject what you have to come to offer me now." However, when Mehmet's brother, İbrahim, passed away in a car accident in 1974 in Italy, Mehmet had to break his promise and attend his brother's funeral in Istanbul. After returning from his brother's funeral, Mehmet told İbrahim Dellal, "What a good choice we made by not going to Turkey and coming to Australia instead." İbrahim added, "Mehmet did not like what he saw in Turkey. Everything from the economic system to the political system bothered him. Moreover, Turkey was influenced by communists who held power at that time, especially at universities."

On January 14, 1950, Mehmet Aceyoğlu, his wife, three daughters, and surviving brother, İbrahim, arrived in Melbourne, thus end-
ing their seven year journey. They stayed at a refugee camp and faced
difficulties. Mehmet landed a job which paid £7 per week, although he
had to travel a long distance to reach the job site. His wife continued
working as a seamstress using the sewing machine given to her by
Prince Amir İbrahim.

The family looked for rental homes, but they were refused
because they had three children. After saving up money, Mehmet purchased land in St. Albans, which was far from Melbourne. He did not
have enough money to purchase building materials. Instead, he purchased wooden cargo boxes and built his two-bedroom cottage using
those. Next to their house, they opened a corner store that was staffed
by Mehmet's wife. She also held bake sales to raise money for Preston
Mosque.

Mehmet, Asiye and İbrahim Dellal met the son of one of the last
Afghan camel drivers. He was an amiable man, and became a good
friend of the Aceyoğlus. I asked for his name. "Mr. Khan" said İbrahim
and Asiye. Neither of them knew his first name. "Everyone called him
by that name," they said. She brought out an antique tray given to
them by Mr. Khan, who received the tray from his father. I examined
this tray. On the back, I noticed some writing etched into the metal
tray. It read, "Gift from Jack Bourne, 1957." I pointed this out to her.
She had not noticed it before. Both Asiye and İbrahim were surprised.

After putting some thought into it, İbrahim suggested that Mr.
Khan may have had a second Australian name. In the 1950s, when
the White Australia Policy[37] was still in effect, most Muslims adopted

---

[37] The White Australia Policy is a set of several policies that restricted the immigration
of non-white people into Australia from 1901-1973. It was first intended to prevent immigration of Chinese and Pacific Islanders who supplied cheap labour.
Dominant political parties wanted to keep Australia as an Anglo-Saxon commonwealth. The legal end in 1973 was by the Labour government led by Prime
Minister Gough Whitlam.

an Australian name, while using their original names among family and friends. Mr. Khan probably had the name etched on the tray by someone else, so he used his official Australian name, "Jack Bourne." İbrahim felt no need to do so since he was a British subject and is light skinned.

Mr. Khan would participate in community activities, such as fundraisings. He aided in the fundraising efforts for Preston Mosque. When things didn't work out the way he wanted with the mosque, he withdrew from the mosque altogether and did not come to Friday prayer. He was a man of sensitive nature, according to İbrahim. It may be that there was a cultural clash between Mr. Khan and the immigrant Muslims. Mr. Khan was born and raised in Australia, so his expectations and customs would differ from the immigrants.

Mehmet Aceyoğlu passed away in 1978, 28 years after arriving in Australia. In those 28 years, he and his wife became good friends with the Dellal brothers. Mehmet's dedication to the community and perseverance mirrored İbrahim's. Mehmet had greeted the first group of Turkish immigrants in Melbourne in 1968, and worked with the Dellals to help the immigrants settle. "He would give his days and nights, and even the weekends, helping the newcomers," said his wife. From running the English course to translating official documents, he was always busy. Aceyoğlu helped to establish the Preston Mosque, Coburg Mosque, Thomastown Mosque, and Prahran Mosque. His friend, Imam Fehmi, led Mehmet's funeral prayer at Preston Mosque, but could not hold his tears back during and after prayer.

There is much more in the Aceyoğlus' lives, especially in their long journey. However, a few times during our conversation, Asiye requested not to have certain details documented. Although it felt like such a loss to ignore the particular things she told me, I held back out of my respect and consideration for her grievances. Sadly, Australia will miss out of the greater story of the Aceyoğlu family, but they will not join the ranks of great Australians who passed away with their stories untold.

1956 Melbourne Olympics

In 1956, İbrahim and his brother Hasan served as official interpreters for the Turkish wrestling team during the Melbourne Olympics. Among the competitors were the successful wrestlers, Yaşar Doğu and Celal Atik, who coached Hamit Kaplan and other wrestlers. The Dellal brothers spent whole days with the team, wanting to take every opportunity to spend time with fellow Turks. Although most of the team did not win gold, Hamit Kaplan won one gold medal.

During Kaplan's last match, he won the gold. During the match, Turkish fans were on the edge of their seats. The two trainers' phrases of encouragement riled up the two dozen Turks in the arena so much that the Turkish cheers seemed louder than all the other voices. İbrahim remembers them shouting, "Haydi yiğidim! Haydi arslanım! Kaldır, yere vur! (Come on, son! Come on, my lion! Lift him and throw him on the ground!)" Hearing the cheers brought much needed enthusiasm to Kaplan.

The next few minutes remain fresh in İbrahim's memories. After several moves, Kaplan turned his rival and threw him to the floor. The trainers were overwhelmed by the success. They ran towards the ring and yelled, "Jump down, Hamit!" They kept calling to Hamit with arms wide open, wanting to share their joy. As Hamit stood to prepare to jump out of the ring, İbrahim feared that the trainers would collapse under Hamit's weight. Hamit jumped into Yaşar Doğu's arms, knocked Yaşar back slightly, but grasped his trainee and fellow countrymen well.

The rest of the Turks were bursting with happiness. Some were even crying out of joy. İbrahim added, "That day had been one of the happiest for the Turks in Australia."

After the Olympics ended, the Dellal brothers led the Turkish group on a tour of Melbourne. They enjoyed the tour and the new sights, but wondered at how the Dellals and the other Turks could live in a land without many other Turks. Dellal admitted that is was difficult, but he had become used to it and did not experience much language difficulties.

It was a bittersweet moment when the Dellal brothers waved goodbye to the Turkish team that was returning home. İbrahim shed tears as they were departing. Left alone with his brother, their loneliness intensified. (PICTURE 5)

CHAPTER 5

İbrahim's Marriage

İBRAHİM'S MARRIAGE

İbrahim's parents wanted to find a suitable girl for their son to marry. To find a proper spouse for one's son or daughter is a custom in traditional Muslim society. According to a tradition established by the Prophet Muhammed, a child has three major rights upon his parents: 1) to receive a proper name with a beautiful meaning; 2) to receive a proper education and upbringing; and 3) to find a marriage partner for the child when he or she reaches an appropriate age.

İbrahim's parents located one possible spouse for their son, but after listening to the conditions for marrying her, İbrahim refused the match. "I did not want to sadden my parents with my rejection, but I could not accept the match," said İbrahim. At that time, İbrahim was working at the post office. Sheila Chapman, his future wife, was working as a secretary at the post office. She was a polite, well-mannered, and honest Irish girl. The young persons felt a great respect and love for one another.

Sheila asked İbrahim to dinner at her home so that she could introduce him to her parents. İbrahim saw that her parents also had her kind nature and were supportive of education and culture. Her father was a builder and her mother was a housewife. "They were good people. They loved me as a father and mother. I felt the same towards them and showed them respect. Since my parents were overseas, I saw her parents as my parents and not just as in-laws," recalled İbrahim.

İbrahim sent a letter to his parents telling them about Sheila and his intention to marry her with their blessing. His parents approved, saying, "If you believe you can be happy together, then you have our blessing to marry." Sheila also talked to her parents, who had approved met with İbrahim and approved of him. İbrahim and Sheila married in 1957. İbrahim's parents were not present at the wedding.

İbrahim had moved out of his brother's house the previous year and settled into a home a few houses down at 12 Palm Street, Reservoir.

Despite their differences İbrahim never forced his wife to accept his belief system or accept the Islamic faith. Sheila joined Muslim community activities and would fundraise with other Muslims through garage and cake sales to raise money for the mosque and needy persons. The couple lived happily. They had three children, Julide, Najiye, and Zerin. Dellal and his wife did not have major conflicts about the amount of time he was spending on community projects. Indeed, Sheila respected and supported him.

THE CYPRIOT TURKISH SOCIETY

Turkish Cypriot Muslims first settled in Australia in the late 1940s. The island of Cyprus was a British colony and its residents were British subjects. The Turkish Cypriots who came at this time were mainly skilled tradesmen. The small community of Turkish Cypriots which arrived in the late 1940s and 1950s was settled by the time the first wave of immigrants from Turkey arrived in the late 1960s. The established Turkish Cypriots were able to mentor and support the new arrivals.

In the 1950s, political tension and violence between Turks and Greeks in Cyprus grew. The siblings were worried about their relatives back home. Except through the occasional letter from relatives, the Turkish-Cypriots in Australia had little news of the events unfolding in Cyprus, and letters took months to arrive. They heard of Turks being harassed and killed in Cyprus. The Turks in Cyprus then established a resistance organization called the *Turk Mukavemet Teskilati* (Turkish Resistance Organization) (TMT) in 1955. It was later revealed that TMT was funded and supported by Turkey's National Intelligence Services (MIT) with the aim of preventing Greek annexation of Cyprus.

For five years, the Dellal bothers had informally discussed the possibility of forming a Turkish Cypriot association in Australia. There were approximately 150-200 Turkish Cypriots living in Australia, and they were scattered across the country. They saw how the

Greeks, including the Greek Cypriots, who were abundant in Melbourne, had formed their own cultural societies and religious organizations. Listing Ahmet's home as the organization's address, the Dellal brothers formed the Cypriot Turkish Society in 1956, with Ahmet serving as President. İbrahim became the president in 1959. They were only a handful of people, but they believed they could do something to help Cyprus through grassroots efforts.

There were a few dozen Cypriot Turks at that time in Melbourne. The Dellal brothers worked to gather their countrymen, but the Cypriot Turks couldn't give time or resources to the Society, and some were simply not interested. It was not easy for members of the society to meet due to long distances and lack of transport. Not everyone owned a car then.

They purchased a building in Carlton where they would meet. Since there was no mosque in Carlton, the building was used for both Friday and Eid prayers. This is when İbrahim first met with Imam Fehmi al-Naja. His acquaintance with Imam Fehmi would open the doors for İbrahim to meet other Muslims later on when he was the head of Islamic societies and his relationship with Imam Fehmi allowed him to be more active in serving the Muslim community.

One of their first outreach events was at the Moomba Festival in Melbourne. Moomba means "out of darkness" in Aboriginal language. The annual event was initiated in 1955 by the city council as a bid in order to liven up the city and attract residents and tourists. Like other festivals, there were carnival rides, parades, and ethnic performances. Over the years, the event became more colorful as it attracted corporate sponsors. The Cypriot Turkish Society made a banner and took part in the parade. The Society also participated in Anzac Day memorials. (PICTURE 6, 7, AND 8)

The Society members wrote letters to politicians and newspapers as a way of lobbying for Cyprus and Turkey. Occasionally, the members would meet with Australian politicians, especially after the 1960s when pressure against Turks in Cyprus was on the rise.

In 1960, İbrahim's parents came to Australia to visit their children. They spent most of their ten-month visit at İbrahim's house, happy to spend time with Sheila and their grandchildren. They appealed to İbrahim to return to Cyprus and take over the family business since they were aging. İbrahim said he would think about it, but was not able to go to Cyprus when the ethnic conflicts escalated.

PLANE CRASH AND THE EXECUTION OF ADNAN MENDERES

Among the Turkish prime ministers that served during his lifetime, Adnan Menderes holds a great respect in İbrahim's heart. On 18th February, 1959, Australian newspapers reported that the Prime Minister's plane, a Turkish Airliner carrying a party of government officials from Istanbul, crashed outside London a few miles short of the runway. The Prime Minister had sustained only minor injuries, possibly because he was sitting in the rear. Of the 24 passengers and crew, only 10 survived. The Prime Minister was on his way to sign the London Agreements on the Cyprus issue. The crash was investigated and found to be caused by technical problems.

İbrahim was relieved to hear that Menderes was still alive because he believed that Turkey was in great need of a leader like him. He defended the political and social rights of the Turkish minority in Cyprus, something which the previous party, the *Cumhuriyet Halk Partisi* or CHP (Republican People Party), did not do during their 28-year administration.

Approximately fifteen months later, on 28th of May, 1960, İbrahim heard on the post office radio that the military had overthrown the Turkish government and had arrested Menderes and leading party members. They were charged with violating Turkey's constitution. İbrahim was shocked by the news. İbrahim saw the coup as a threat to the developing democracy in Turkey. He knew that human rights would be trampled on and that economic conditions would deteriorate under military rule. Moreover, Turkey's international reputation would be smeared. He returned home depressed, and Sheila did her best to console him.

When İbrahim arrived at work, his coworkers enquired for information regarding political developments in Turkey. Unfortunately, İbrahim had little information to share. Every day, İbrahim listened to the radio and read the newspapers to learn more. Due to the technology of the day, news outlets would have limited information to report.

Menderes was later sentenced to death and executed on September 17, 1961, despite pleas from world leaders such as President John F. Kennedy and Queen Elizabeth II. İbrahim heard the news the day after Menderes was executed. He felt it to be one of the worst days of his life. He wondered how a politician who had secured the people's support could be executed. Even in his last Parliament election, his party won 408 of the 500 seats. Following Islamic tradition, İbrahim said, "*Allah rahmet eyelsin*" or "May God grant him mercy," which is said after a person dies. "Whenever I remember Menderes, I ask God to have mercy on him and feel sorrow for his execution. He was compassionate, hardworking, and a people's man. He wanted to develop democracy in Turkey and give more freedom to people," said İbrahim. However, Menderes did not live long enough to carry out his dream.

İbrahim observed, "His greatness can be easily understood in many aspects. Look at the letter he wrote as his will before he was executed."

> *I don't have a grudge you [the executors]. I know which masters are holding you and the other leading figures' strings. I don't have a grudge against them either. When you take my corpse to them, tell them that Adnan Menderes is grateful that you did not kill him when he began working for freedom and democracy 17 years ago. There is no reason for my execution. Would you be able to tell your living heroic masters who live in the shadows of weapons that I went to death with fortitude? Let me say this as well. I could have saved you and your masters with the freedoms that would be gained as a people as I did in 1950 [via elections]. You should not have feared my living self. However, the people will follow up on you for eternity as to why Adnan Menderes died, and,*

one day, will wipe you off the face of the earth. Yet, despite this, my prayers are with you.[38]

His words echoed in the public's mind when Cemal Gürsel, leader of the military coup responsible for overthrowing Adnan Menderes and putting him on military court, suffered paralysis and died less than a year later. The committee that led the coup fell into dispute and did not win majority of votes in the next election.

A person who even forgives his executioners and those who made that decision is full of God's love. To İbrahim, Menderes was the political version of Rumi[39]. Rumi had once received a letter full of hate, and the sender had asked why he loved the sinner and the saint, Muslim and non-Muslim alike. Rumi replied with the statement, "Come, there is room in my heart for you too."

Because of İbrahim's love of God and love of people, regardless of who they are, Rumi is naturally his favorite poet. İbrahim adores Rumi's poems about God, love, humanity, and mysticism. Whenever İbrahim went to Turkey, he made sure to visit Konya, the last residing place of Rumi. It is called the City of Rumi, since his tomb is located there. İbrahim said, "When I visited his tomb, I recited the first chapter of the Qur'an, and prayed two *rakaat* (cycles) at the nearby mosque. Near his tomb there is a museum where Sufi music is played. I went to listen to that and it made me feel serene. I listen to Sufi music from time to time for relaxation and contemplation."

İbrahim explained the appeal of Rumi, saying "Rumi's spiritual attractiveness for centuries and his influence over people, including non-Muslims, shows his magnificence." Below are some excerpts from Rumi's poetry that İbrahim indicated were among his personal favorites.

---

[38] http://www.biyografi.info/kisi/adnan-menderes

[39] Mawalana Jalal ad-Din Muhammad Rumi (1207-1273) was a 13th century Persian poet, mystic, Islamic jurist and theologian. His poems have been widely translated. BBC news has called him "the most popular poet in America." Rumi has always been an incredible love singer and he is held as one of the great spiritual masters and mystic poets of Islamic civilization. Rumi's teachings are universal in nature. They are based on an urge to come closer to God through love.

Love is from the infinite, and will remain until eternity.
The seeker of love escapes the chains of birth and death.
Tomorrow, when resurrection comes,
The heart that is not in love will fail the test.

With the Beloved's water of life, no illness remains
In the Beloved's rose garden of union, no thorn remains.
They say there is a window from one heart to another
How can there be a window where no wall remains?

Do you want to enter paradise?
To walk the path of Truth
You need the grace of God.
We all face death in the end.
But on the way, be careful
Never to hurt a human heart!

If I love myself,
I love you.
If I love you,
I love myself.

ISLAMIC SOCIETY OF VICTORIA

In 1957, the Islamic Society of Victoria was established in Preston. In 1962, they elected İbrahim to be president of the society via a unanimous vote. İbrahim stated that he was not worthy of such a position, but the board members pointed out his English language capabilities. Board members included Lebanese Imam Fehmi Naji, Pakistani Dr. Abdul Khaliq Kazi, Bosnian Jalal ad-Deen, Bosnian Suleyman (whose last name İbrahim can't remember), Mehmet Aceyoğlu, Albanian Farid Yamrer, and his brother, Ramadan.

Dr. Kazi recalls how the Muslims in Victoria did not have a house of worship. They would perform the congregational Friday prayer in university classrooms or at the Cypriot Turkish Society. Since he was a well-known Muslim, Dr. Kazi would receive phone calls from time to time for advice and help. He said, "I received calls from the grandchildren of the last Afghan camel drivers to help perform the funeral, even though I was not an Imam. Once, at an Afghan man's funeral, I was asked to wash the deceased's body. Sheikh Fehmi was at Lebanon at the time. I had never performed this rite before, and did it to the best of my knowledge."

For Dr. Kazi, this request was also disappointing. The men who made that request were only Muslim by name, but knew "almost nothing" about Islam. It was a sign that the Afghans who had come in earlier years could not pass on cultural and religious values. This fueled the desire to have a mosque and Islamic centre to educate the Muslim children.

Another purpose of the Islamic Society of Victoria was to establish relations with other Muslims in Australia. The board members traveled to Adelaide to meet with Muslims residing there. They spoke with Imam Ahmet Skaka, a Bosnian Imam who arrived in Australia after World War II as a refugee. There were only a handful of Muslims living around Adelaide's humble mosque at that time. İbrahim met with Imam Ahmet a few times. Imam Ahmet assisted and advised AFIS during the Society's earlier years. Like Mehmet Aceyoğlu, Imam Ahmet passed through difficulty before and after immigrating to Australia. Author of *Muslims in Australia*, Bilal Cleland describes Ahmet Skaka's life story (based on a personal interview):

> Ahmet Skaka, trained as an imam in Sarajevo, enlisted in the Yugoslav Army then imprisoned by the Nazis in Stalag 17 in Bosnia and escaping to Brno at war's end, sought emigration to Australia which was, at that time, eagerly seeking suitable settlers. He sailed for 26 days from Napoli to Melbourne, arriving on January 26 1950 and was transferred to the migrant settlement camp at Bonegilla. On the ship to Australia, he recalls, there was not one Bosnian. The passengers were mainly Italians, Romanians and Poles. In Bonegilla there were a few Russian Muslims and a few Romanian Muslims. They were able to get halal food from a family of Albanians who had a farm not far from the migrant camp. In accord with the terms of his migration he was assigned a job and equipped with an Employment Certificate which stated that the bearer had to remain in the assigned employment for 2 years. Ahmet Skaka and a Romanian Muslim from the camp were

assigned for two years to the same job, at Clipsall in Adelaide. Both of them assumed that Adelaide was a desert so far as Islam was concerned.

They only discovered that there was a mosque in that city from a newspaper report of the death and funeral of Gool Mahomet. The following Saturday they set out to find it. There was a congregation of only two or three aged Afghans. From then on Ahmet acted as imam of the mosque while continuing to work for Clipsall. Only 7 people attended the Eid Prayer in 1951. All the old Afghans continued to wear national dress and when the younger ones, born and brought up in Australia, came to the mosque in European dress, the old men called them non-Muslims. Imam Skaka told of an incident which occurred after Colombo Plan students started to come to study in Australia. One young Malaysian student brought a Quran in Latin script to the mosque. The 80-year-old caretaker, Iset Khan, finding it sitting inside, declared it a kaffir (non-believer) book and threw it out, onto the ground. Ahmet Skaka had to explain what it was.

Iset lived in the little room in the backyard of the mosque. He refused electric light and used a kerosene lamp, giving permission for the introduction of the godless innovation only when the lamp blew up. He had come to Australia when he was a young man[40].

According to Imam Skaka, the non-Muslim residents living near the mosque on Little Gilbert Street in Adelaide were very hopeful that the Muslims would vanish with the last Afghans and that the land would come up for sale. However, the demise of the White Australia Policy caused them to lose hope.

It was interesting for İbrahim to hear what Muslims in Adelaide experienced since it was central for the Afghan camel drivers. While Imam Ahmet arrived in Australia around the same time as İbrahim, he knew more about the camel drivers due to his being in Adelaide. İbrahim said, "He told me important stories about the last camel

---

40 Bilal Cleeland, The Muslims in Australia: A Brief History, Islamic Society of Victoria, 2002, Melbourne, p.69-70.

drivers whose lives were full of sadness and joy, but I can't remember them. I wish I had written them."

FORMING THE AUSTRALIAN FEDERATION OF ISLAMIC SOCIETIES (AFIS)

Dr. Kazi and the other Muslims felt that the Muslims needed a representing body in Australia. Dr. Kazi said, "We needed one voice to show Australia who we Muslims are and what we stand for. We wanted to familiarise Australia with Muslims. What also triggered us to form AFIS was the need to have a Muslim marriage celebrant."

Ibrahim, Dr. Kazi, and Sheikh Fehmi had already formed a network with other Islamic Societies in New South Wales, Queensland, South Australia, Capital Territory, and Western Australia, and they called for a gathering of representative in Melbourne.

In 10 of May, 1963, the first meeting of the Australian Federation of Islamic Societies (AFIS) was held at the University of Melbourne where Dr. Abdul Khaliq Kazi was a lecturer. 15-20 people were present from five states. Dr. Kazi had prepared the AFIS's constitution. He was later elected as president. Ibrahim was vice-president, Dr. Nasih Mirza was a board member, Sheikh Fehmi was elected as secretary, and Jalal Deen was the treasurer. Their duties included providing halal meat, organizing religious holiday activities, and bringing Muslims together. They worked with local and federal government officials on meeting the needs of Muslims in Australia.

One of the problems within the Muslim community that was discussed at the first meeting was the lack of communication between Muslims living in different regions of Australia. To address this issue, the board began publishing *The Minaret Magazine*, a publication reporting the ongoing activities of Muslims in Australia. Rashid Craig, an Australian who later accepted Islam, was given the task of editing and publishing. They printed 500 copies a month and distributed them without charging readers a fee. (PICTURE 9, 10, AND 11)

To meet their goals, AFIS members decided to get into contact with governments of Muslim countries, particularly the Gulf countries. Other issues on the agenda included registering AFIS as an official umbrella organization, and applying for more space in cemeteries for Muslims.

During his years working for AFIS, İbrahim faced the misconception of some non-Turkish Muslims who believed that the Turks had abandoned Islam after the collapse of the Ottoman Empire and after Atatürk's reforms had been instituted. In their opinion, İbrahim was an exception. As much as he tried to convince them otherwise, İbrahim failed to change their impression of Turks until Turks began immigrating to Australia in large numbers.

As in any organization, argument and division was common, whether it was over the location of potential mosques or the use of funds. Naturally, cultural differences were also a factor in the disagreements. Despite this, the organization grew and gained strength over time.

CHAPTER 6

İbrahim Becomes a Key Player in
Turkish Immigration to Australia

İBRAHİM BECOMES A KEY PLAYER IN TURKISH IMMIGRATION TO AUSTRALIA

I brahim was invited to give a speech at the Good Neighborhood Council city branch[41]. At that time, İbrahim was the president of the Australian Federation of Islamic Societies (AFIS). İbrahim provides details about that memorable day:

> Most of the audience members were female. After my speech, they proceeded to ask questions. The way they asked seemed very sincere, making them unforgettable. One question was, "Are Turks like you?" I answered, "Our appearances vary, but in the aspect of being hardworking, honest, righteous, and having high moral values, we are alike. Our way of life is similar." The audience looked pleased with the answer. Another person asked, "Are there communists among you Turks?" I had little communication with Turkey since I arrived in Australia and had little knowledge about politics in Turkey at that time, I gave a short reply. "As far as I know, there aren't because Turks have faith in God. A believer can't be a communist." This answer pleased them as well.
>
> I was asked to speak before them again. They later asked me to serve as the consultant for Immigration Services. The GNC met with Immigration Minister, Bill Snaden, to suggest that the country bring immigrants from Turkey to settle in Australia. Through

41 Good Neighborhood Councils were formed by members of churches, Country Women's Associations, Parents and Citizens committees, youth and returned soldiers' organizations, Rotary and many other voluntary bodies to integrate immigrants and promote their desire to become Australian citizens. GNC began with the Citizenship Convention in January 1950, and continued to be funded by the federal government through the 1960s and 1970s in order to help immigrants settle in a country that needed laborers to rebuild post-war economy through secondary industries. GNC had branches all over Australia staffed by workers and volunteers. *www.multiculturalaustralia.edu.au/doc/deptimm_3.pdf*

this position, I volunteered to bring Turkish immigrants. The Turks had a good reputation in Australia based on the positive accounts of ANZAC soldiers. I also prayed to God for Turks to come to Australia. My prayers were answered.

On the 28th of October, 1964, sixteen years after his arrival on Australia's shores, İbrahim was granted his Certificate of Registration as an Australian Citizen from the Commonwealth of Australia. He had not applied for citizenship after he first arrived in Australia since he was uncertain about his future. Years passed before he realized that he wanted to continue his life in Australia.

On October 5, 1967, the Australian Immigration Minister, Bill Snadden, traveled to Turkey to sign an agreement allowing Turks to enter Australia in great numbers. According to the statements on the Republic of Turkey's Ministry of Foreign Affairs website, the agreement, consisting of 29 articles, included the establishment of an Australian office in Ankara to organize immigration since Australia did not have an ambassador in Turkey until 1968.

However, Snadden returned without signing the agreement because the Turkish government did not want to send Turks as immigrants, but rather as guest workers. On the minister's second trip, it was agreed that Turkey would recognize the Turks as guest workers when they departed for Australia, but Australia would recognize them as immigrants.

Occupational categories recruited were mainly semi-skilled craft and production process workers, and unskilled labourers. Although the agreement aimed for an intake of 30 percent skilled and 70 percent unskilled, in the early years of the program, most of the workers were unskilled.

Attempts to attract Turkish professionals as part of the assisted passage arrangements were only partially successful. "Loss of caste" was reported as one of the reasons why professionals were reluctant to apply. Turkish authorities seemed unwilling to help, forcing Australian representatives to work "through the back door", securing professional migrants through alternative contacts.

ANOTHER TURNING POINT

Official immigration from the Turkish mainland did not begin until 1968 with the advent of the Australian-Turkish Assisted Passage Scheme[42]. This bilateral agreement was signed in 1967. Between 1968 and 1971, thousands of Turkish families arrived, increasing the number of Turks in Australia from 1544 to 11,589[43]. The total Muslim population increased to 22,311. The scheme marked a turning point in the history of Muslims in Australia.

The Australian economy needed workers for its expanding manufacturing industries in Melbourne and Sydney, and there was a decline in the number of British immigrants. Unlike existing guest worker schemes in Europe, the Australian program encouraged Turks to bring their families and settle permanently. It was hoped that wives would also work outside the home in local factories[44].

PERSUADING THE TURKS

Some of the Turks who had at first agreed to emigrate would change their minds at the last minute. The Australian government sent İbrahim to Turkey to investigate the matter. İbrahim met with many of these Turks and tried to determine their reasons for not coming to Australia. He was surprised with some of the answers he received. One Turkish man had been frightened by stories about cannibals in Australia. One Turk feared that the distance between Turkey and Australia would keep him away from Turkey forever. Some were worried about Turkey's reputation in Australia after the Gallipoli Battle. They asked İbrahim about the climate, housing, food, and culture of Australia.

To persuade the hesitant Turks, İbrahim described the better life that awaited them in Australia with its beautiful lands and business

---

[42] (http://uncommonlives.naa.gov.au/contents.asp?cID=98) accessed 13 of February, 2009

[43] http://uncommonlives.naa.gov.au/contents.asp?cID=98&lID=9 accessed 13 of February, 2009

[44] http://uncommonlives.naa.gov.au/contents.asp?cID=98

opportunities, and remarked that they had the chance to return to Turkey if they wished. He answered their questions patiently, and succeeded in decreasing their fears of the far-away land.

The first Turkish group arrived in Sydney on the 14th of September, 1968. İbrahim travelled 15 hours by car to Sydney to greet them. He had prepared a small welcoming banner that wrote *"Hos Geldiniz* (Welcome)" to catch the attention of the new arrivals, express the support of his organization, and communicate to the new arrivals that they had friends in Australia. At the airport terminal, he could not believe his eyes. The Cypriot Turks from Sydney also came to greet the newcomers[45]. The arrival section resembled a sea of colors; Turkish flags and banners filled the room.

At the airport, İbrahim met with a blind man who was in his wheelchair, waiting to greet the immigrants as well. İbrahim recalled:

> His name was Mustafa. I called him Mustafa *Amca* (Uncle Mustafa). It was the only meeting I would have with this man. Mustafa Amca was one of the Ottoman Turks who came with the Afghan camel drivers. He was pleased that more Turks were coming to Australia. When the immigrants finally arrived, they did not have their baggage checked by customs officials because of the Turks trustworthy reputation. Mustafa Amca asked me, "Did they arrive?" I replied in the affirmative. He put his head low and began crying. "All thanks be to God that Turks came to this country before I died, just as I had prayed for years."
>
> I asked him what he had prayed for. He gave me some advice, and then said, "I used to live in Adelaide with other non-Turkish Muslims. We were about 3-4 people. One day, we all prayed to God together. Crying, we said, 'God, please send the Muslims here before we die." In 1946, we were in a mosque with other friends. We heard some footsteps. The door opened and four youths stepped in. The other men asked, "Mustafa, are they here at last?" I said, "Yes." Seeing the four Muslim youths, we could not hold our tears back. We thanked God because he answered our prayer.

---

45 Hussein, Serkan & Carusu, Edward, Yesterday & Today - Turkish Cypriots of Australia,

I prepared some tea and breakfasted with those youths. When I asked for their names, the young men told me their names were Hasan, Hüseyin, Ali, and Mehmet. We had not heard such names in a long time. They told us their stories. Two of the men were Bosnian, while the other two were from the Caucus. They had lost their families in World War II and fell prisoner. After the war, they immigrated to Australia.

These young men settled in Adelaide. They made renovations to the mosque, painted its walls, and cleaned the yard. The other elders and I passed on the duty of taking care of the mosque to these young men. We wanted to hand over the mosque and all its belongings to them. At first, they did not want to accept out of humility, but later conceded.

We told them, "We have been praying for years for young men like you to come and take care of this mosque. Some of us never married, had no children, and died. Others had children, but they did not take care of the mosque. We begged God not to take our lives until young Muslims arrived here. One of us even saw your coming in his dream. We have been awaiting your arrival for a long time. You too will hand over this to others." See, İbrahim, the Turks are coming now. God has answered our prayers. Even if I die, my heart will not be left behind.

Mustafa Amca cut off his story when the immigrants started coming through customs. He asked, "How are their *fez* and vests?" He still thought that Turkish men wore the *fez*. He had no idea about the fall of the Ottoman Empire. "Are they wearing Trablus garb waistbands?" He had heard from others that Turkey had changed completely, and was curious to know if that was the truth. "How about their appearances? Are they tall?" İbrahim replied to him, "Don't worry, Mustafa Amca. They are just as you wish." He smiled and said, "That's great. The Turks are just as they were when I left them." That is all I remember of Mustafa Amca. I do not know what happened to him afterwards.

At the end of the welcoming festivities, İbrahim returned to Melbourne to greet another Turkish immigrant group. He immediately invited the newcomers to a Turkish dinner hosted by the AFIS. The atmosphere was jovial as a few men had brought their *saz*, a Turkish lute used for folk songs. They proceeded to sing well-known *türkü*, or folk songs, joined by İbrahim. The guests felt welcomed and connected to their new country.

In 1971, İbrahim traveled to Turkey as an interpreter to facilitate the process of bringing more immigrants to Australia. Together with the immigrants on the plane, İbrahim witnessed the declarations of a Turkish bureaucrat. He said, "We are going to a civilized country now. Take off your headscarves. It is a disgrace for you to be wearing these things there." İbrahim could not tolerate this man's words, especially when he repeated them. He approached the man and said, "Enough is enough. This is Australia. Democracy is practiced here. No one bothers anyone whether they wear the headscarf, dress or not." This silenced the bureaucrat. (PICTURE 12)

CAUCASIAN TURK CEMAL NAZLI

Mehmet Aceyoğlu was also at the airport to greet the newcomers. Aceyoğlu was a Caucus Turk. Cemal Nazlı, who was among the newly arrived Turks, relates this story[46]. "In Mehmet's welcome speech to the immigrants, he spoke about a dream he had 11 years ago. He dreamed that the Turks were immigrating to Australia. Tears rolled down his face when he said, 'Allah accepted my prayer.' Mehmet was also one who was praying for years for the arrival of the Turks to Australia. He added that 'the hard days had passed', and the coming days will hold much joy."

Over a period of two years, approximately 4000 Turks arrived in Melbourne and Sydney. Their arrival made the rest of the Turks in Australia happy. The Herald described the newcomers in a short passage. "Their hearts were full of courage for they were descendants of

---

[46] Suleyman Unal (Aksiyon, 575, 12.12.05) Erdoğan'ın Ziyareti Münasebetiyle, "On the Visit of (Prime Minister) Erdogan"

the brave soldiers of the Crimea and Gallipoli, and they knew the terrors of earthquakes and famine in their own unlucky country[47]."

Because of the respect between Turkish and Anzac soldiers that grew out of their wartime encounters, the Australian public had a better image of Turkish Muslims in comparison to other Muslims.

Nevertheless, the first generation of Turkish settlers in Australia faced the same problems that all immigrants from non-English speaking nations face (e.g., lack of affordable housing and employment, language barriers, dealing with an unfamiliar culture, and occupational health and safety issues). Within a decade, a range of institutions and services had been established to improve the lives of Turkish immigrants reflecting the determination of "a community that was here to stay.[48]"

Housing Cooperative

As with other immigrants, the Turks experienced much difficulty. Perhaps their greatest impediment was the language barrier, making it difficult to find work and to communicate in order to satisfy their basic needs. The immigrants found it hard to adapt to the dietary habits in Australia. Furthermore, the change from living in rural homes to crowded hostels caused them distress and homesickness. They were not able to meet all of their needs with the meager savings they had brought with them.

While the government aimed to attract immigrant workers who would eventually settle, the typical Turkish immigrant's intention was to live in Australia long enough to earn money and then return to Turkey. They were therefore careful how they spent their money. Initially, some families rented homes and lived together. Sometimes, there would be two families or three couples residing in one house. In overcrowded homes, disagreements, arguments, and even fistfights

---

[47] *Herald*, 13 February 1971
[48] Manderson, L "Turks' in James Jupp (ed.), *The Australian People*, Angus and Robertson, Sydney, 1988, pp. 818-25

occurred in the household, leading to great discontentment among the Turks. This gave the Turks a negative image both in the neighbourhood and in the media. "I was afraid that the bad reputation would lead the Australian government to stop bringing immigrants from Turkey," added İbrahim.

İbrahim realized that many of the problems experienced by the immigrants could be solved if they had their own homes. He joined with other Turkish Australians and established a housing cooperative in Preston. İbrahim told Dr. Kazi about this project like he was describing a vision. İbrahim wanted to form something like a Muslim village which would have its mosque, school, butcher, and other facilities that met the need of Muslims. Dr. Kazi hesitated to support this idea. He said, "We were afraid of becoming more vulnerable if we were all in one place. If the Australian government were to go back to its White Australia days, or become even more intolerant, the 'Muslim village' would be an easy target, almost like the Jews were in Nazi Germany. In later years, I realized that İbrahim had a great idea. İbrahim is a man with many visions. There are always community projects in his mind. He's a very positive and optimistic man."

In addition to aiding the Turks, he had another objective. "I wanted to show Australia that the Turks were here to stay." The cooperative borrowed $250,000 from the state government. The cheque was issued to the cooperative and the Premier Rupert (Dick) Hamer handed the check to İbrahim.

It was not long before a rumor spread that İbrahim was using the money for his own purposes. While İbrahim did not expect praise, he never thought that he would be subjected to such slander. İbrahim explained, "First, the cheque was issued to the cooperative, not me, and was deposited in the bank. Second, with this money, we made 16 homes in Preston. The family would give $2,000 deposit, and pay $155 monthly. When the Turkish community saw the fruits of our work, they were embarrassed for speaking ill or harboring any doubts."

With the cooperation of real estate agents, the first house in Thomastown sold for $11,580, with a $2,000 deposit. Rent was around the same as weekly payments. In thirty years time, it would be possible for immigrants to pay off this mortgage and own a home. A new home was being sold once a month. After the first two to three years, the number of Turkish immigrants coming to Australia grew and housing prices soared from the original $11,000 to $25,000-30,000 per home.

Sadık Yurtsever immigrated to Australia on the 23rd of March, 1969. With the encouragement and support of İbrahim, he purchased a house in Thomastown in October of the same year. Sadık paid a deposit of $850 for his house, and eventually paid off an $11,000 mortgage. "I was one of the first to buy a house among the Turkish immigrants," he said.

Other Turks approached Sadık regarding his purchase of a house, and asked him about if he intended to live in Australia permanently. Sadık stated that he trusted İbrahim's judgment and followed his advice. Moreover, he added, "I was not a practicing Muslim prior to my arrival here. It was İbrahim who took me to the mosque, taught me how to pray, and made me familiar with God and Islam." İbrahim cared for the individual's material and spiritual needs.

According to Sadık, İbrahim's encouragement and support helped 30 individuals to become homeowners. He would take the immigrants to realtors, drive them to see various types of houses, and be their translator at every step of the way. He guided them to banks or mortgage companies, explained the procedures and the contracts clearly, and showed them what needed to be done. He would spend three to four days for the purchase of one house since none of the buyers could speak English. It was a weary task to spend hours after work and on weekends to serve the Turkish immigrants, but İbrahim found it spiritually rewarding to help those in need.

On occasion, İbrahim would take time off from work in order to help the newcomers. His nights and weekends were devoted to the growing Muslim community. Sadık relates a few stories that illustrate not only İbrahim's commitment to others, but the kind-heartedness of his wife, Sheila.

The day we moved into the house, we had nothing, not even beds. Next thing we knew, İbrahim came with two beds in a truck. It was a weekend. His wife, Sheila, came with hot lentil soup, together with some bread, bowls, and utensils. That soup was better than a million dollars. I was really touched and always recall reminiscently Sheila's great hospitality the day I moved in. She was not Turkish herself and did not even know me, yet she made Turkish-style food for me. I will always value and treasure that memory.

Whenever I had a problem, I would always call İbrahim first. One day, around dinnertime, my wife and I could not find our son. We searched for him in the house, around the house, and in the neighborhood. We could not find him. He was just a toddler. My wife was crying. We were terrified, not knowing what to do, especially in a new country. We called İbrahim, who came right away. İbrahim called the police, and together, they looked for my boy. Two hours later, the police and İbrahim found our son about a kilometer away at a construction site. It looked like he played a while and then fell asleep.

Another time, I was in Mildura and needed an interpreter. My son had a car accident and had to appear in court. I called İbrahim. He left work, and drove six hours to Mildura to attend the court session, and then returned back immediately.

İbrahim not only helped others, he also encouraged others to do the same. On one occasion, İbrahim invited Sadık for a fundraising dinner for Işık College[49] in 1997. Sadık said, "I came with the intention of giving maybe $50 or $100 max. I saw that İbrahim pledged a great amount, as did many others on that night. I was so impressed and inspired that I pledged $5,000. Since then, I have become used to giving large amounts in charity."

Sadık is convinced that İbrahim could not have done it alone. Sadık observed:

When Sheila came into the house the day we moved in, she saw that our curtains were too short. She took the curtains home,

---

[49] In Australia, the term "college" refers to primary and secondary schools (K-12).

bought extra material similar to the curtains, and lengthened the curtains. If Sheila was not so kind-hearted and patient, İbrahim could not have done all that he did. He gave much of his time, even the time he should have spent with his family.

To me, he was like a parent, both a mother and a father. With his help, twelve of my relatives came to Australia[50]. We would go together to the right office, get the right forms, and fill them out together. He would always follow up on the progress of their cases, ensuring that everything was going well.

Some people even thought that İbrahim received some commission for each person that he helped purchase a home, Sadık explained:

People asked, "If he is not doing all this for money, then why is he doing this?" I have known İbrahim for almost 40 years, and whenever someone else or I called him, I don't remember him refusing. Moreover, despite all that he had done for my family and others, he would never accept any money, not even petrol money. I have no doubt that İbrahim helped many others as he helped me, but he would not tell others. Both he and Mehmet Aceyoğlu would go to whatever mosque or organization needed help and offer their services.

I asked Sadık, "What motivates İbrahim to do so much?" Sadık replied:

There are many reasons, but I think that he wanted our children to have a better future and not experience the same difficulties his children experienced. Helping people is a part of his life. He is a patient man full of hope, a man of his word, and values every person that comes to him. Even when people accused him of many things, and at one stage took legal action against him, he forgave them.

Not all appreciated İbrahim's efforts in helping new arrivals purchase homes. They suggested that İbrahim had a hidden agenda of establishing a permanent Turkish population in Australia, whereas the immigrants had intended to stay only a few years to earn money.

---

[50] The Australian government gave the immigrants the right to apply for permanent visa for their relatives abroad. This policy ended in 1974.

İbrahim had enough experience with the Turkish immigrants who intended to leave after a few years to know that they would settle eventually, so he did not take the criticism to heart. He explained that the house purchase was not forced upon them, and provided them with an investment that would benefit them in the long run, regardless of whether they chose to stay or leave after a few years. He pointed out that his efforts were voluntary and sincere, refuting any criticism of being an opportunist. His only goal was to make the settler's transition easier.

English Course

İbrahim tackled the language barrier issue with a volunteer-led English language program at the AFIS building. İbrahim's older brother, Ahmet, would even use his car to pick up the settlers and take them to English classes after their long workdays. There would be separate classes for men and women. There were no other existing classes that catered to the language needs of the Turkish community at that time. A local TV station interviewed İbrahim and the immigrants three months after the classes began. The reporter was surprised at the progress made. *The Herald* reported that five courses were offered in Fawkner, Moonee Ponds, South Melbourne, Preston, and Thomastown. İbrahim said that approximately 100 to 130 individuals attended the classes.

Reporting for *The Herald*, Brian Gill quoted İbrahim stating, "When my people come here, I remind them that when you plant a tree, it will not bear fruit right away. It is the same with any newcomer to Australia. He has to adapt to new customs, learn a new language. It takes time. I have worked my way up from my first job here in a garage. Now I have everything I could ask for. I want it to be the same for all the Turkish immigrants who have followed"[51]

After the news was out on both TV and in newspapers, representatives from local government visited the AFIS centre to learn more.

---

[51] *The Herald*, 29.Aug.1970

They too were surprised at the rate that the immigrants, who worked 8-10 hours a day, picked up the language. İbrahim and the other volunteers were so confident in their endeavor that they welcomed anyone to strike up a conversation with their students.

İbrahim and his friends believed that immigrants would not be successful until they gained command of the English language. They had seen just how much hardship the Turks unable to speak English went through, and had experienced similar problems themselves.

Sadık told me how İbrahim believed in being blessed for helping those who were alone and without support of relatives and friends. He arranged marriages for single people, including widows. İbrahim spoke of how there were ten single men that came in one group. He helped them settle at a hostel, and later came to visit them. İbrahim recalled:

> They were in a pitiful condition. They did not know how to take care of themselves properly. They couldn't cook food or clean their clothes well. They asked me to set up marriages for them, if possible. I told them that I would think about it.
>
> I contacted the Immigration Department whose bureaucrats I had good connections with. I requested that they specifically bring ten extra women in the next group of immigrants because there were ten single men who needed wives. It was nearly impossible to find a compatible wife for those men in Australia, given the cultural divide. The person in charge at the Department laughed at my request, but agreed. They made sure to include ten single women in the next group.
>
> Before the women boarded the plane for Australia, I received a call from the person in charge, confirming that ten women were on their way, and that it was my responsibility to meet them at the airport and help them settle at Young Christian Women's Association's (YCWA) hostel. I did what was needed. I then proceeded to helping them find jobs, and arranging language classes.
>
> One day, when went to visit them, I saw that they were arguing among themselves. I spoke with each of them separately. In about three to five months, I set up consensual marriages for eight of the

ten women with the men in the hostel. The remaining two women were already engaged, but their fiancés were in Turkey. I asked for the necessary documents for them, and arranged for their fiancés to come to Australia within a few months. I am still in contact with some of these men and women.

Mehmet Aceyoğlu led the English language classes. Having arrived in Australia in 1950, he quickly mastered a sufficient level of English in one year and began teaching science at local schools. When he heard of the immigrants coming to Australia, he admitted to İbrahim that he wanted to aid the newcomers and protect them from the same difficulties he had faced. These words of Mehmet still bring pleasure to İbrahim when he thinks about it. He remembers Mehmet being active in teaching and interpreting until his death in 1978.

Although they were from different countries, İbrahim regarded Mehmet as a *hemsehri*, or "fellow countryman," a term used widely among the Turks. He shared his feelings of homesickness and his love for serving the community with İbrahim. When Mehmet fell ill towards the end of his life, İbrahim visited him in the hospital. Mehmet's words were carved into İbrahim's memory. Mehmet said:

> İbrahim, İbrahim listen to me. For years, the communist regime struggled to dissolve (i.e. assimilate) us (Turkic culture and family), but we did not dissolve. As a family, and as a community, we always remained together. We acted as one body. We brought their plans of dissolving us to naught. We were defiant against many difficulties. However, I see that the system here (in Australia) is different. This place can assimilate us very subtly and very easily, as there is no oppression here. Here though assimilation is still sought, yet in a gentle and jovial way. Yes, because of this, there is a great problem here, so we must live and work accordingly in order to continue our way of life and beautiful values.

> Our mosques and schools must be established quickly in order to educate our descendants in the most beautiful manner, with affection, kindness, clemency, gentleness, and love so that they will be able to serve this community, and if needed, all humanity. Because our way of life is very beautiful, meaningful, reasonable, and desperately needed by humankind. Therefore, this way of life must

not die. It must be lived and kept alive. We are the only ones who can do that here. If we don't, there is no tomorrow for us.

THE TURKISH NEWS

While Turks today enjoy numerous methods of communication with relatives back home and hear news regarding Turkey, these methods were very limited in the 1960s due to the technology. Not knowing what was going on back home generated a great deal of anxiety for the settlers. Seeing that they had a desire for news of Turkish events covering both the local and international scenes, İbrahim and his circle of friends began publishing *Turk Sesi* (the Turkish Voice) with the English title *The Turkish News* fortnightly, and, eventually, weekly. Community news such as notices of meetings, marriages, births, deaths, celebrations, and classified advertisements were included. It also included a half to full page section called "Let's Learn English." The first issue was published in 1970, and it continued to appear until 1996. Despite the fact that it was not financially profitable, they continued to publish the newspaper. İbrahim's wife Sheila would help write the English section of the newspaper.

Ibrahim said that he gathered news of Turkey by listening to the radio. However, this method was unreliable since reception was often poor and weather-dependant. To compensate for that, İbrahim and the others writing for *The Turkish News* would make use of other news sources and translate the news into Turkish. (PICTURE 13)

POLITICAL INVOLVEMENT

The Turks at that time were sharply divided into politically right and left. Just like in Turkey, the division was very deep and visible. They would have different organizations, cultural centers, and even newspapers. Even though he is considered right wing, İbrahim did not discriminate between the left and right when it came to helping fellow Turks.

When I asked İbrahim about his involvement in politics during the 1970s, İbrahim mentioned Sir John Grey Gorton as someone he supported. Sir John was the prime minister during the late 1960s when İbrahim worked on bringing Turkish immigrants to Australia. İbrahim approved of Sir John and admired some of his policies. "Sir John was humble and considerate of the people," İbrahim said. This led İbrahim to join the Liberal Party. Moreover, İbrahim thought well of Bill Snaden, the Minister of Immigration.

İbrahim also spoke well of former Prime Minister Edward Gough Whitlam and his Minister of Immigration, Albert Jaime Grasby. They both encouraged immigration from non-English speaking countries and abolished the White Australia Policy in 1973.

İbrahim made it clear that, although he had joined the Liberal Party, he did not support just one party. He said on one occasion, "Whoever emphasizes education, indiscriminately serves the people of Australia, maintains honesty throughout through humility, and acts as an ordinary citizen, will receive my support and vote. This kind of a politician works as the 'people's man' and strives with the cabinet for the steady progression of the nation."

İbrahim was not interested in politics personally. He would vote for whichever party seemed to benefit the community and country the most. In 1965, he became a member of the Liberal Party in order to further help the community through a different channel (i.e., politics). He did not know at that time that his membership would open doors and allow him to reach out to senior members of the Liberal Party and help Turks settle in Australia. He had contacts and correspondence with different parties and party members at both local and federal levels. After he began heading organizations (such as the AFIS), he became more valuable to politicians. "During my most active days in politics, I helped Tayfun Eren, a local Turkish immigrant, to be elected for the local legislature," observed İbrahim.

İbrahim has also been critical of political parties from time to time. He criticized former Liberal government Trade Minister Simon Crean's anti-terror law. When İbrahim had an opportunity to speak with Minister Crean at a community gathering, he told him that "with this law, you make all Muslims potentially suspicious." In 2007, when the Labour Party won the majority of seats, a local Liberal Party bureaucrat asked İbrahim whom he voted for. İbrahim responded, "This time, I voted for the Labour Party. Before this, I have voted for the Liberal Party." The bureaucrat then asked İbrahim why the Liberal Party lost the election. İbrahim replied, "Some Liberal leaders waged war together with neoconservatives in the US against the last religion, Islam. God then took away the power from the Liberals and gave it to others."

CHAPTER 7

İbrahim in the Media

İBRAHİM IN THE MEDIA

"MUSTAFA MAKES IT"

After the Turks began migrating to Australia in large numbers, İbrahim established housing cooperatives. His goal was to ensure that the Turkish immigrants became homeowners. Alan Stewart from *The Herald* covered this development for Weekend Magazine (13.Feb.1971). At that time, he interviewed İbrahim about the project. İbrahim said, "No matter how well educated a man is, when he migrates to a strange new land, he is like a child. He is anxious and frightened." Knowing this motivated İbrahim to help his fellow countrymen.

İbrahim told the new immigrants, "This is a good country and a free country. It is up to you whether you make your life here heaven or hell." He advised the Turks to find lodging close to their jobs so that they would not have to buy a car, and warned them not to spend too much money on purchasing furniture. He advised that "they should instead save as much as they can, and invest in a home." He also added, "The children [of the immigrants] will be the adult Australians of tomorrow. The seed of the tree must be planted well if it is to bear good fruit," referring to the education of the children.

"WE'RE A TURKISH DELIGHT"

On 29 August, 1970, *The Herald* reported that when Coburg Councilor Allan Lugg complained about Turkish immigrants having been dumped in Coburg, and neglecting their children while they worked, İbrahim came to the defense of the Turks. "My people are good people. They are not like those immigrants who sit in hostels and grizzle about their new country. They go out after jobs and make a success of them. They are hard workers, hard savers, and many of them have their own homes within 12 months of their arrival," observed İbrahim. He further responded to the councilor's comments regarding Turks settling in Coburg. "Why condemn one race? Don't other new arrivals from other places do the same thing?"

İbrahim told *The Herald* reporter that he would visit his parents in Cyprus. He was quoted as stating that "my visit will be evidence to the people at home that my migration has been successful. I hope to encourage more Turks to come to Australia. But always, I will be reminding them that it rests only with themselves to make a success of their new life." Regardless, İbrahim said, "You might say that I want them [immigrants] to find Australia a Turkish delight."

"ISLAMIC MARRIAGE CEREMONY IN AUSTRALIA"

One of Turkey's leading daily newspapers, *Hürriyet,* reported an Australian story on the front page. The article, entitled *"Avustralya'da Imam Nikahi* (Islamic Marriage Ceremony in Australia)" was written by Beria Cetintaş. The article, dated 20 August, 1969, covered the first Islamic marriage ceremony involving the 1968 wave of immigrants.

Imam Skaka in Adelaide had previously applied to be a marriage celebrant in 1955, but was denied. The matter was taken to the court, where it was denied again. When İbrahim had assisted Imam Fehmi in applying for a certificate to be a marriage celebrant, they gained the certificate they wanted. It was another sign that Australia was opening its arms wider to immigrants.

Imam Fehmi performed the ceremony. Since İbrahim was the president of the AFIS at that time, he hosted the couple at the Islamic Society of Victoria's center. Özgen Gülten and Gönül Kantul, who arrived only two months earlier, decided to marry in Australia instead of taking an expensive trip to Turkey. The news was broadcast on television as well, showing an interview with İbrahim about the event.(PIC-TURE 14)

Picture 1: İbrahim on the left, father Hasan Hüseyin,
and older brother Ahmet on the right

COMMONWEALTH OF AUSTRALIA.

APPLICATION FOR PERMIT TO ENTER AUSTRALIA.

(Immigration Act, 1901-1935).

Notes.—(1) If the applicant is residing in the British Isles or Europe this form should be forwarded to—

The Official Secretary,
Australia House,
Strand,
London,
England.

If the applicant resides elsewhere the form should be forwarded to—
The Secretary,
Department of Immigration,
Canberra,
Australia.

(2) This Application must be filled up in the English language, and the Certificate from a qualified medical practitioner, police officer or other public official, if not in English, must be accompanied by a certified translation in that language.

Full Name—
Surname to be stated in block letters.
Address.

I, **Ibrahim Hussein DELLAL,**

of **7, Ikkindji Selim street, Larnaca, Cyprus,** do hereby make application for permission to enter Australia, and in support of the application submit the following information, which I declare to be true :—

(1) Full name **Ibrahim Hussein DELLAL,**

(2) Nationality **British Subject by Birth,**

(3) Race **White** (State also whether Jewish or not **Not Jewish but Mohammedan**

(4) I was born at **Scala, Cyprus** on the ~~day of~~ **the 13th day of August,** 19 **32**

(5) Marital status (single, married, widowed or divorced) **Single,**

(6) I shall be accompanied by the following members of my family :—

unaccompanied by fs and ildren ite "Travelling Unaccompanied."

—	Name	Sex	Date of Birth	Birthplace
	TRAVELLING UNACCOMPANIED.			
Wife ..				
Children {				

(7) My last place of permanent residence was **7, Ikkindji Selim st. Larnaca Cyprus.**

(8) My present occupation is **Mechanic,**

(9) My proposed occupation in Australia is **Mechanic,**

[P.T.O.

Picture 2: İbrahim's official document at arrival

Picture 3: İbrahim and author standing in front of Mohammedan Chapel

Picture 4: Mehmet Aceyoglu in 1944

(Above) The Turkish Olympic Wrestlers in their formal uniforms at the Olympic Village in Heidelberg

(Left) Hasan Dellal on the left, walking with the Turkish Olympic Wrestler Yaşar Doğu (right) at the Olympic Village in Heidelberg

Picture 5: Courtesy: Hussein, Serkan & Carusu, Edward. *Yesterday & Today - Turkish Cypriots of Australia*. PromozPlus, Melbourne. 2007

(Above) The Cyprus Turkish Association members in their costumes representing Turkey at the Moomba parade. The Turkish Cypriots have always portrayed their love for Turkey and their Turkishness and worked to be the representatives of both the Turkish people of Turkey and the Turkish Cypriots (1961)

Picture 6: Courtesy: Hussein, Serkan & Carusu, Edward. *Yesterday & Today - Turkish Cypriots of Australia*. PromozPlus, Melbourne. 2007

(Above) Hasan Dellal holding the wreath is surrounded by fellow Turkish Cypriots at the Shrine. The wreath was placed to commemorate ANZAC day on behalf of the Turkish community and the Republic of Turkey

Picture 7: Courtesy: Hussein, Serkan & Carusu, Edward. *Yesterday & Today - Turkish Cypriots of Australia*. PromozPlus, Melbourne. 2007

Picture 8: Eid celebration at Cyprus Turkish Society in 1957

Picture 9: First AFIS board (from left to right): Jalal Deen, Dr. Abdul Khaliq Kazi, Sheikh Fehmi, Dr. Nasih Mirza, and Ibrahim Dellal

Picture 10: Cake for Eid celebration

Picture 11: The cover of Minaret Magazine

Welcome address to first group of migrants from Turkiye to Melbourne.

15ᵗʰ October 1968

Picture 12

Picture 13: Cover page of *Turkish News*

Picture 14: Marriage covered by Hurriyet in the first page in Turkey

Er meydanı

Thomastown Türk İslam birliğinin düzenledi-
ği Yağlı güreş, halka açık ilk cayır antren-
manı yapılmıştır. Göçmen bakanlığı (Victoria)
müdürü ile diğer hükümet ilgililerinin yanı
sıra 2 ve 0 televizyonunun filme aldığı ön
gösteri mahiyetindeki karşılaşma heyecanla
izlenmiştir. Resimde kapışan iki pehlivan gö
rülmektedir.

Picture 15: Oil Wrestling in Thomastown in 1972

Picture 16: Ibrahim receives Silver Medal from one of the
members of Federal Parliament

Picture 17: Ibrahim with former Australian Prime Minister Bob Hawke

Picture 18: Ibrahim with Turkish Prime Minister Recep Tayyip Erdogan

CHAPTER 8

Tension in the Community:
The Coburg Mosque

TENSION IN THE COMMUNITY:
THE COBURG MOSQUE

U ntil 1971, Preston Mosque was the only one located in the greater Melbourne area. İbrahim was the head of the mosque, leading it with Dr. Kazi and Imam Fahmi. After the Turks arrived, they came to the mosque on Fridays for prayer and on weekends to receive help from İbrahim. Problems ranged from translating documents, immigration and legal issues, and conflicts within the family, İbrahim observed:

> When more and more Turks started coming to the mosque and becoming members, the other ethnic groups felt uneasy. They felt like the Turks were going to take over. One particular ethnic group was feeling that unease. Due to the lack of a common language, the ethnic groups could not communicate well. They began eying each other with suspicion and sharing their fears amongst themselves.
>
> I was worried. If things continued as they were, conflict could break out, especially among the narrow-minded persons. I spoke with Dr. Kazi and Imam Fahmi about this. I told them that it would be best if I quit. That way, fewer Turks would come to the mosque. I was thinking that establishing a new organization to help the Turkish immigrants might be a good idea. At first, Dr. Kazi, Imam Fahmi, and some other members disagreed. They thought that my resignation and idea of a new organization would split the community.

Dr. Kazi remembered the smallest details around this tension. He said:

> The Turks were noticeably different. They would pray the sunnah (extra) prayers in the mosque, and use prayer beads to invoke

God's name. They were more disciplined with their movements and positions in the mosque. They expressed their disappointment at the more relaxed behaviour of others. The Turks were already beginning to overcome the other ethnic groups in numbers. If they all assumed membership, they would take over the board. This is what the others felt.

The Turkish immigrants in Coburg then formed the Coburg Turkish Islamic Society (CTIS). İbrahim declined to be a board member, but served as an advisor when needed. Since he had maintained his relations with Preston Mosque, he did not want to deepen the split. The president was İbrahim Şimşek, who was later killed in a car accident. The CTIS purchased two timber houses in 1971 to use as a mosque and religious study centre. İbrahim was a guarantor for CTIS together with Mehmet Aceyoğlu, a Caucasian Turkish Muslim.

The Muslims began using the premises for Friday prayers and small weekend classes. They had not yet received permission to use the building as a mosque. The neighbours were against having a mosque in their area out of fear of an immigrant group and worry that it would devalue their homes. İbrahim visited those neighbours living near the building the CTIS had purchased to persuade the residents that they had nothing to be concerned about. Again, his mastery of the English language and familiarity with Western customs and manners aided him in solving this issue.

İbrahim knew his actions would be understood in time. "Later, Dr. Kazi and Imam Fehmi saw the benefit of the split. Another mosque was built, and the congregation grew. An ethnic conflict in the Muslim community was avoided, but relationships continued under the umbrella of AFIS, and later, AFIC (Australian Federation of Islamic Councils)."

The two small buildings were not spacious enough to meet the needs of the Muslims. In 1976, the new Fatih Mosque Complex, also known as Coburg Islamic Centre, was completed at 31 Nicholson St. The centre sought to truly reflect the needs of the local Muslims.

The congregation was divided on mosque leadership. On one side was the *Milli Görüş* group, a politically active Islamic group whose members supported Necmettin Erbakan, a popular Islamic political leader in Turkey who would later become prime minister. The military pressured Erbakan to resign in 1997. On the other side were a mix of different Turks, including secular Muslims, pro-Atatürk[52], and non-partisans. The power struggle, especially in the mosque where Muslims are meant to unite, was contrary to İbrahim's nature as a bridge-builder, so he withdrew from the congregation and ended his support.

İbrahim also assisted Western Thracian Turks in the purchase of a building and helped establish a new mosque in 1974. He was a guarantor because they did not have enough funds to obtain a mortgage from the bank. The Western Thracian Turks were from northeastern Greece and southern Bulgaria and had settled in Prahran, Victoria. They wanted to establish a mosque. They held meetings in one Thracian's garage until they purchased a building.

While İbrahim was volunteering for the mosque and Islamic societies, he was labelled by secular Turks as *dinci*, which literally means "religious person," but is used to refer to a fundamentalist. Some political Islamists viewed him as pro-Atatürk who supported the anti-religion secular system. İbrahim's friend, Orhan Çiçek, saw that İbrahim did not take these labels to heart and kept his focus on serving the community.

TROUBLE AT THE HOSPITAL

One night in 1970, İbrahim received a phone call. It was a Turkish man he was acquainted with. When this man's wife fell ill, he took her to the hospital in a taxi. However, the man, being a new arrival, did not speak English. He called İbrahim and said "İbrahim, my wife is sick. I'm at the hospital. The hospital staff are swearing at us! I'm going to bash these people! Is this any way to treat a sick person and

---

52 Those who are pro-Atatürk are generally secular Muslims who support separation of religion and state and are known to be fervent nationalists.

her husband? Please come and help me." İbrahim replied, "Take it easy. Don't do anything. Wait for me. I'm on my way."

İbrahim arrived at the hospital. He saw the man's wife in pain. İbrahim learned that she had not received medical attention yet. The Turkish man was at odds with a male staff member who looked bewildered. İbrahim spoke with the male employee who said, "I have no idea why they are angry! I'm trying to help them. I was going to call for an interpreter, but I need to get some information for the records first before the treatment. I asked them, 'What is your sickness?' He got angry at me. It's a good thing you came."

İbrahim laughed, and explained why the Turkish man was angry. "The word 'sick' in Turkish is a swear word that refers to the male private parts. Since you asked the wife, the husband became extremely angry." The staff member looked shocked, and then relieved. He said, "I'll make sure not to use that word next time then."

When İbrahim explained the meaning of the word to the Turkish man and his wife, they both felt embarrassed at their lack of English and the misunderstanding they caused. "We really need to learn this language quickly," said the Turkish man. "It's a good thing you came. Otherwise, I would have fought with this man." It would not be wrong in Turkish culture if he had fought with the male staff member. In a culture that highly values personal and bodily privacy, especially for women, such a statement could easily cause a conflict.

This was not the first or the last of such incidents for İbrahim. Communication problems were common, and often lead to serious situations. Now, İbrahim can laugh at these memories since the former settlers learned English and newer immigrants have an easier time learning English and there are more people to help them master a second language.

THOMASTOWN TURKISH ISLAMIC SOCIETY

In 1970, İbrahim helped the Turkish Muslims in Thomastown to organize a religious group. They formed the Thomastown Turkish

Islamic Society and wanted to build a mosque as a long-term project. However, they had no funds. At the board meeting in 1972, it was suggested that they hold a fundraising event called *yağlı güreş* (oil wrestling) that would attract other Turks. *Yağlı güreş* is a national sport in Turkey. Wrestlers cover themselves with olive oil and aim to knock the opponent to the ground. The match is won when the opponent's back hits the ground. İbrahim published information about the upcoming event in the Turkish News.

The event drew on a number of traditional customs such as Ottoman clothing as well as the davul (kettledrum) and the zurna (clarion), two instruments often used to promote an event and increase excitement. It worked to attract local non-Turks as well. It is customary to offer the winner of the wrestling match a ram. In the fundraising event, however, the ram was auctioned off. It was sold for ten times the normal price. The event drew a lot of people and was profitable, pleasing the organizers. Indeed, two reporters from local TV stations covered the event. Representatives from the Department of Immigration were also present. (PICTURE 15)

FIRST RETURN TRIP TO CYPRUS

In 1971, the Australian government sent İbrahim to Turkey to act as an interpreter for a new group of Turkish immigrants. İbrahim took the opportunity to travel to Cyprus by plane and visit his parents. When he arrived at Nichosya airport, however, he was detained for nearly eight hours. The tension between Turks and Greeks was still high, and the airport was controlled by the Greeks. He was interrogated and then freed.

İbrahim took a taxi to his parents' home in Larnaca. It was 10pm when he arrived, surprising his parents a great deal since he had not informed them that he was coming to visit. He stayed a few days with his parents. After conversations with his father and neighbours, İbrahim realized hoping for a peaceful Cyprus was futile. Most of the Greek Cypriots voted for *enosis*, union with Greece, while the Turkish Cypriots were against it. This lessened İbrahim's desire to return.

Even İbrahim's parents did not try to convince their son to stay because he was more secure in Australia.

He went to Yeni Mosque in Larnaca to pray the noon prayer. There he encountered a few acquaintances. They told him their grievances. Their sheikh, Sheikh Nazım, was imprisoned for giving a sermon without the consent of the secular Turkish political leaders in the Cypriot government.

Cyprus was not divided into two states. According to the constitution, the president would be Greek and the deputy president would be Turkish. İbrahim recalled his meeting with the deputy president. He said, "I knew the deputy, Rauf Denktaş, since my childhood. I agreed to help my friends. I visited Denktaş and enquired about the matter. Denktaş ordered the release of the sheikh."

Sheikh Nazım belonged to the order of Naqhshbandi, a major Sufi branch. After his release, he invited İbrahim to breakfast in his *tekke* (Sufi lodge) in Nichosya. The lodge was very simple. There was a thin mat on the floor. Breakfast consisted of olives, cucumbers, yogurt, and bread. The Sheikh invited İbrahim to stay a few days at the *tekke*, but İbrahim kindly declined because he had business in Turkey. İbrahim and the Sheikh parted ways.

TRIP TO MUNICH AND SECOND TRIP TO CYPRUS

In 1973, İbrahim, while serving as president of AFIC, received an invitation to attend a mosque opening in Munich. The Libyan government had built the mosque. Using his own money, İbrahim purchased tickets for flights to both Munich and Cyprus. In Munich, he met with the Libyan foreign minister Mansur Kikhia. Upon meeting the president of AFIS (Australian Federation of Islamic Societies), the Libyan minister said, "You don't look Australian." İbrahim replied, "I'm a Cypriot Turk who immigrated to Australia." İbrahim narrated his life story and his work helping Turks settle in Australia.

The Libyan minister informed İbrahim that Libya had reached an agreement with the Cyprus government to bring 3,000 skilled guest workers to Libya. İbrahim said, "The government in Cyprus is under Greek control, so they will send only Greeks. Here is my card. Let's see if we can arrange for some Cypriot Turks to come as well. If you can not reach me, contact Sheikh Mahmud."

When İbrahim arrived at Nichosya airport, he was again detained and interrogated at the airport. He visited his parents and performed congregational prayers at Yeni Mosque. His friends were pleased to see him, especially since Sheikh Nazım had been arrested again. İbrahim went to see Rauf Dentkas in order to have the Sheikh released.

While İbrahim met with Denktaş, they discussed the Libyan matter. Denktaş stated that approximately 3,000 Cypriot Turks had recently graduated from universities in Turkey and were looking for stable employment. Moreover, many of them were communists (as a result of their education in Turkey, where universities were under the control of communists or supporters of left-wing political parties). İbrahim saw a perfect opportunity for these skilled graduates in Libya, which was mainly a socialist a country. Denktaş was a bit apprehensive about sending communists to Libya. However, İbrahim assured Denktaş that everything would work out, saying, "They will go as communists, make money, and return as capitalists!" Denktaş later informed İbrahim that his prediction came true. The workers, being exposed to a socialist system, did indeed return as capitalists.

Before İbrahim left Denktaş, he made a request. "Release Sheikh Nazım again. What crime did he commit that he is detained?" İbrahim asked. "He's a *dinci* (religious fundamentalist)." This surprised İbrahim, who replied, "He is a Sufi. They cannot be fundamentalists. They don't bother with politics or use force." Refraining from political involvement and remaining non-partisan is a Sufi tradition. Dentkas ordered the release of the sheikh.

Sheikh Nazım invited İbrahim to the Sufi lodge. At the door of the lodge, there was a man who warned İbrahim about visiting the sheikh. "They may arrest you too," the man said. "But I have committed no crime, so why should I worry?" replied İbrahim as he entered the building.

İbrahim reproached the Sheikh for wasting his efforts in Cyprus when there was a greater need abroad, especially in European countries. "You can speak English, Arabic, and Turkish. Why don't you go to England? The people there are in more need of spiritual services. Despite your efforts here, you have few people around you, and you face constant persecution." The sheikh liked the idea, and said, "Let me think about it for a while." İbrahim stayed at the Sufi lodge for two days. The morning after his arrival, İbrahim was approached by Sheikh Nazım, who said, "The decision was made. I am leaving today for England."

İbrahim wondered what the sheikh meant when he said "the decision was made." In Sufi practices, when a major decision needs to be made, a Sufi either asks the master of the Sufi order or will make a certain supplication, and sleep waiting for an inspired dream. Since his response came the next morning, the sheikh may have had a dream that indicated that the proposal was auspicious.

It was not long before someone knocked on the door. It was Yagci Hussein, a wealthy businessman, who was probably a follower of Shaikh Nazım. He exclaimed, "Sheikh, your ticket is ready." It was a one-way ticket. İbrahim said, "After that, I did not meet the sheikh again. However, he always sends his greetings with anyone who comes to Australia." İbrahim's advice to the sheikh was a fateful one. After traveling to England, the sheikh opened a Sufi lodge in London. He then went on to establish Sufi lodges in other European countries, and in the US. He became a major force in spreading the Naqshbandi order in Western countries, and became a global spiritual leader.

MEETING THE ICONIC ROCK SINGER

I entered İbrahim's office to ask him some questions about his biography, only to find him listening to Barış Manço, a popular and internationally known Turkish rock singer [53]. I was surprised since I thought

---

53 Barış Manço (1943-1999), is a Turkish rock singer, composer, television producer, celebrity, popular icon, and public figure. He composed 200 songs, some of which have been translated into English, Dutch, Japanese, Bulgarian, Persian,

İbrahim was not interested in rock music at his age of 77 years. I asked, "Do you like Barış Manço's song?" He smiled and said, "Of course. Did I tell you about the time…" and I quickly took out my notebook to record another one of his treasured memories.

It was a weekend in 1974 when İbrahim passed by Coburg mosque and wanted to pray there. Inside, he came across a long-haired man. İbrahim was not too familiar with his face since he was detached from the world of Turkish entertainment due to being in Australia. When the long-haired man introduced himself as Barış Manço, İbrahim was surprised. He had heard about the singer, and knew him to be left-wing and supposedly anti-religious. When Manço saw his reaction, he said, "Did you think I was against religion? I have a spiritual side too. Don't look at my long hair. This is the fashion now. I grow it long so I can appeal and reach out the hearts of people."

From their conversation, İbrahim learned that Manço had been invited by the Turks to give a concert. Manço had told the people he was travelling with that he would go off on his own for a while, and eventually ended up at the mosque. At the end of their conversation, İbrahim and Manço shared contact information.

Four years later, İbrahim received a letter from Manço inviting him to his wedding. "I could not go due to my work. Otherwise, I had intended to go," says İbrahim. "He was a spiritual person full of love in his heart. When he passed away, it upset me. He was a man of love and compassion. We can see this in all his songs."

Greek, and Arabic. During the ultra left and ultra right wing conflict in Turkey, he leaned towards the left. With his long hair, moustache, and big earrings, his flower child look worked on the rock scene. He is listed as one of the most influential Turkish musicians, especially due to his contributions to Turkish rock. His music appealed to different people. He produced rock, but his themes were universal on ranged from love to nature. His children songs made him a popular figure. When he passed away, his funeral received great attention on national news and thousands attended. His songs are received as a legacy.

CONFLICT IN CYPRUS

Life in Cyprus had become difficult by the 1970s. Political fanatics in Cyprus pressured the Turkish population to leave Cyprus, thereby turning the island nation into a Greek state. İbrahim would hear from his parents of how their electricity had been turned off for long periods of time by supporters of the Cypriot union with Greece. Their homes were vandalized and the residents were harassed during the night. İbrahim's parents being old and alone could not do much to resist such persecution. They saw these harassments as a psychological warfare. İbrahim's mother, Naciye, died on the day that the Turkish Army took control of Northern Cyprus in 1974. The cause of death was never established since İbrahim's father, Hasan Hüseyin, and brother, Hasan, who was visiting at that time, did not have time to call a physician or take her to the hospital.

On the day of her death, Hasan Hüseyin, Naciye, and Hasan woke to the sound of bombs. They feared that the worst was happening. After being under political pressure for some time, they thought that some sort of warfare was being launched against the Turks. They immediately turned on the radio to hear that the Turkish Army had entered Girne, a city in Northern Cyprus, and the Greeks retaliated. There was fear that Greek Cypriot army and rebels might retaliate by hurting the Turks living in Cyprus, especially those in the south. When the bombing began, the Dellals prepared to evacuate. Hasan Hüseyin went to his wife, only to see her fall to the ground. She had died. The battle on her homeland was very stressful and may have triggered a heart attack.

Since the bombing continued, Hasan Hüseyin and his son, Hasan, has to quickly bury Naciye, fighting the immense pain in their hearts and wiping the tears from their eyes. They took shelter at the British army barracks. Through the Red Cross, Hasan was able to fly to London, and then to Australia, whereas his father was transferred to northern Nicosia, the current capital of Cyprus, where the Turks were in control. He did not join his sons in Australia because he didn't want to leave his homeland.

When İbrahim heard of the combat taking place in Cyprus, he grew anxious. He was eager for news about his parents and brother. He couldn't reach them by phone and was unable to communicate with them in any other way. He turned to God and prayed for his family's safety. "What else could I do at that time except rely on God's help?" said İbrahim. His belief in God gave him the patience and hope he needed. He was devastated when he later heard about his mother's sudden death. The Turks and Cypriot Turks in Melbourne visited him to express their condolences. Hearing that his father and brother were safe gave him much needed relief. When he visited Cyprus in 2005, he desperately searched for his mother's grave, but could not locate it. This has remained an unresolved pain in İbrahim's heart.

His father stayed in a nursing home on the Turkish side of Nichosia where he passed away in 1978. He faced the pains of loneliness, homelessness, and the ultimate sadness of losing everything he had known and loved. He had left his house with only the coat on his back. He had no time to gather much else during that invasion.

The news of his father's death hurt İbrahim greatly. He followed the Islamic tradition of having relatives and friends over to read from the Qur'an and pray for the deceased[54]. İbrahim's close friend, Imam Fehmi, and a Turkish imam came as well. İbrahim's neighbours brought food which is also a custom in the Muslim community[55].

---

[54] Prophet Muhammad, peace be upon him, said, "A deceased person awaits for dua from a relative."

[55] The Prophet asked his Companions to take food to the deceased person's house for seven days after the death. The purpose is to aid the grieving relatives during the difficult time by checking on them daily and ensuring that they do not skip meals by eating together. This way, the grieving person knows that he or she has support. This custom is less common among non-practicing Muslims.

Umrah Trip

İbrahim performed the Umrah four times and the Hajj once[56]. His first Umrah was in 1975. "I cannot find any word to express my happiness at that time. I felt like I was in a dream," said İbrahim. When he visited the Prophet's Mosque in Medina, Saudi Arabia, and met a Circassian sheikh (Circassia **is** a region in southern Russia). İbrahim recalled:

> Back then, I did not have much knowledge about Islam. The sheikh told me to go pray at a certain spot in the mosque because the Prophet had prayed there. He added that if a sincere Muslim prayed there, he would shed tears while he prayed. I went and began to pray in that spot he indicated. I cried throughout the prayer. I felt as though I had abandoned this life and was living in the next life.
>
> Around that point, I had a vision. A group of people dressed in white with light on their faces were looking at me. They smiled and said, "Welcome." I did not know who they were, but I felt some peace within by just looking at them. I had similar visions in Mecca and in other places in Medina with the same people. I would get a scent of flowers during the vision. I wasn't scared when I saw them, but rather felt something strengthening within me.

AFIS Becomes AFIC

In 1974, Dr. Kazi took his sabbatical leave and travelled to Saudi Arabia. Since he was a graduate of Al-Azhar University, he spoke Arabic well. Through his network, he was able to secure an appointment with King Faisal bin Abdul Aziz al Saud (1904-1975). He talked to the King about the state of Muslims in Australia, the benefits of living in

---

56 The Hajj is the obligatory pilgrimage to the Ka'bah, the most sacred mosque and the direction of the five obligatory daily prayers. The Ka'bah is located in Mecca, Saudi Arabia, the birthplace of Prophet Muhammad, peace be upon him. The Hajj must be performed once in a lifetime by able-bodied Muslims during the last month in the Islamic calendar. The Umrah is the pilgrimage to Mecca that is not obligatory and can be undertaken at any time of the year..

Australia, and the challenges the Muslims faced. Dr Kazi returned to Australia.

A few months later, a two-man delegation from Saudi Arabia arrived in Australia with the aim of helping the Muslim communities become financially stable. In fact, 1.2 million dollars were given by the Saudi government to the AFIS for funding mosques and Islamic centers[57]. Dr. Kazi assumed they were sent by the King. The delegation consisted of Dr. Abdullah al-Zayed, rector of the Abdul Aziz University in Riyadh, and Dr. Ali Kattani (1941-2001), an adviser to King Faisal, former rector of Ibn Rushd University in Cordoba, Spain, and one of the few experts on Muslim minorities. During Dr. Kattani's academic term in the US, the AFIS invited him to visit Australia. After his first visit, Dr. Kattani visited Australia several more times in the 1970s and 1980s, and met with İbrahim and other prominent Muslim leaders.

İbrahim said that Dr. Kattani's roots "go back to the Ottomans. His sister was married to a Turkish man and living in Istanbul. He was educated and taught in both Eastern and Western institutions. He was a sincere man. He especially encouraged Muslims to educate their children and open educational institutions, not just mosques. He did not have radical ideas. He was a man of compassion."

Acting on the recommendation of Dr. Ali Kattani, Islamic councils were set up in each state, and the Australian Federation of Islamic Societies (AFIS) changed its name to Australian Federation of Islamic Councils (AFIC) in 1976. Islamic societies where organized under their state's Islamic council, and the Islamic councils of each state were under AFIC. İbrahim continued in his position as vice president of the AFIC.

One of AFIC's contributions to the Muslim community was providing halal (Islamically permissible) meat. Taking advantage of the business connections between Saudi Arabia and Australia, where the

---

[57] Report of Royal Commission into Australian Meat Industry. September 1982. The Hon. Mr. Justice Woodward Commissioner. AGPS Canberra, 1982, p.221. Cited in Cleeland, p,77-79.

former desired halal meat, AFIC served as a regulator to ensure that the meat was slaughtered according to Islamic rules.

One of İbrahim's great achievements was to persuade officials in Muslim countries, such as Saudi Arabia, Iran, and the Gulf States, to purchase meat from Australia. He traveled with Dr. Kazi to Muslim countries and organized meetings between government officials and business leaders in Australia. Since that time, Australia has sold halal meat and has generated billions of dollars in revenue. A small percentage of that money was given to the Muslim community in Australia to be used to build mosques and educational institutions.

From 1974-1977, İbrahim served as chairman of the halal meat committee of AFIC. İbrahim observed:

> When Australia was engaged in the halal meat trade, Dr. Kattani organized for a very small percentage of the profit to go to Muslim organization in Australia. In the 1970s, the Saudi government alone purchased more than $100,000,000 worth of meat per year, leaving $1,000,000 for Muslim organizations in Australia. Both Australian farmers and Muslim organizations benefited from this trade. Many Muslim organizations were newly established and financially poor since the newly arrived Muslim were blue-collar workers. Since then, Australian meat exporters are profiting from this trade.

The AFIC made certain that the meat was slaughtered according to Islamic rules. The AFIC used the payments from these transactions to fund mosques and Islamic schools. This also expanded the halal meat industry in Australia, making halal foods more available and benefiting Australia's meat and poultry industry.

He saw that Australian meat was more affordable in comparison to meat from many other countries. One additional aim in exporting meat was to support Australian livestock traders. His father had been a livestock trader in Cyprus, hence İbrahim was familiar with the industry and wanted to help. After selling meat to Muslim countries, the AFIC would receive a small percentage of commission in return for regulating standards in the slaughterhouses. This money would then fund the construction of mosques and the establishment of Islamic organizations throughout Australia. This would be of great help to Muslim immigrants who had recently settled in Australia and did not have enough financial resources to build mosques or run schools. Also, since exported meat would be less expensive lower-income citizens in Muslim countries would be able to afford it.

Throughout the three years İbrahim was in charge of maintaining halal standards, some local Muslims accused İbrahim of not properly regulating the slaughterhouses. These local Muslims would write to the ambassadors of the import Muslim countries, criticising İbrahim for poor quality checks. They also saw him as an opportunist, even though he did not receive a salary. İbrahim tried to tolerate the criticism. He recalled:

> I thought they were jealous, or wanted a share in the commission. Sometimes, the differences in the amounts we would give to mosques and organizations were disputed. We could not give equal amounts. We gave according to their needs, and we would give more to those who were under construction. Finally, when a certain leader, whose name I won't reveal, in the Sydney area complained about me to the Saudi Arabian ambassador, whom he had good relations with, I decided to quit. I realized that good works will have great obstacles. I was only able to last three years against these obstacles. I tolerated their accusations, until it was being spread that I was using the money for myself. I couldn't bear this. What's interesting is that the leader from Sydney was exposed as an opportunist himself.

I asked İbrahim and Dr Kazi if the donor had any power to direct use of money or any influence over the decision made in the committee. Both of them replied that there were no such conditions.

JOURNEY TO INDONESIA

In 1975, İbrahim went to Indonesia for halal meat business. He was Vice President of the AFIC at that time. He met with officials in the federal government in Indonesia to discuss halal meat export from Australia. He assured them that the meat coming out of Australia had been prepared according to Islamic principles. This strengthened already existing business relations.

The highlight of İbrahim's trip to Indonesia was the Eid ul-Adha (Feast of the Sacrifice) prayer. Indonesia is the country with the greatest number of Muslims. Hence, stadiums were used to observe the major prayer. İbrahim joined approximately 300,000 Indonesians in a sports stadium in Jakarta for the prayer. İbrahim recalled, "I had never prayed with so many people before. When the congregation said, '*Amin* (Amen)[58]', it felt like the earth and heavens groaned. It was a fascinating experience."

İbrahim also took his family to Indonesia for a vacation. They stayed in Indonesia for one month and enjoyed sightseeing. İbrahim found the Indonesians from all walks of life to be warm-hearted and welcoming.

QUEEN ELIZABETH HONORS İBRAHİM

On 6 June, 1977, İbrahim received one of Australia's highest honours for his contribution to Australian society through the halal meat export and community service. He was awarded the Silver Jubilee Medal by Her Majesty Queen Elizabeth[59]. (PICTURE 16)

MEETING KHOMEINI

After the Islamic Revolution in 1979, İbrahim and three friends, one being a Lebanese Shiite, visited Iran. The aim of the trip was ensure that Australians continued to ship halal meat to Iran as they did during the previous regime. They spoke with the minister in charge of meat imports. They were asked if the group would like to visit Khomeini. İbrahim and his friends accepted the invitation. In the city of Koom, they visited a simple mudbrick house where Khomeini

---

58 The Islamic equivalent of "Amen" is "Amin." It is said in various situations, such as during congregational supplication. In this situation, it was said after the last verse of the opening chapter of the Qur'an recited by the imam.

59 Hüseyin, Serkan & Carusu, Edward p 103

lived. They had a simple breakfast of olives, yogurt, cucumber, honey, and bread with Khomeini on a cloth placed on the floor

When Khomeini learned that İbrahim was Turkish, he spoke in basic Turkish. Khomeini stated, "There will be those who will arouse enmity between the Shiites and the Sunnis. Beware of them. The roots of the Sunnis and Shiites are the same. Sunni means the *sunnah* (tradition) of our Prophet Muhammad, peace be upon him. Shiite means the ally of our the Prophet's cousin Ali. Because Muslims are poor and ignorant, they may fall for the trick. Do not fall for any propaganda that says otherwise."

İbrahim thought that Khomeini was a humble person, especially after seeing his home and his straw mat that served as a bed, together with a pillow and blanket. The people around Khomeini followed a simple lifestyle as well. Khomeini said, "All praise be to God for not giving me the Palace of the Shah." He was grateful that he could live in a simple house because most Iranians also lived in simple houses. In a traditional Islamic society, the leader should have a simple lifestyle like an ordinary citizen. If the leader lives in luxury, there will be a large gap between the leader and the people. This may lead to discontent among the people and lack of support, especially when laws need to be enforced.

The group received a tour of Tehran. Finally, they were told that the import of Australian halal meat would continue, but that Iranian officials would come to Australia to inspect the butcheries and slaughterhouses. İbrahim and his friends left Iran pleased with the way the group had been received. They were treated more warmly than they had expected. Having a Shiite with them was also beneficial because Iranians are primarily Shiite.

Later in the year, a group of Australian livestock companies sent İbrahim to Algeria to speak with the bureaucrats and business leaders in that country. His trip was not successful from a trading perspective, but İbrahim had an interesting experience. When he arrived at the hotel, he noticed that hotel staffers were extremely courteous towards him. This went on for a day or two until İbrahim met a man named Ali who spoke some Turkish.

"Why are the staff treating me special?" asked İbrahim. "They think you are the brother of Algerian President Chadli Bendjadid," replied Ali. Ali even found a picture of the president's brother. "I really do look like him," said İbrahim. He looked up to Ali and said, "Don't tell anyone who I really am. Let them continue treating me as they are now."

MILITARY COUP IN TURKEY: NOT AGAIN!

İbrahim was sitting at home on the evening of 12 September, 1980, enjoying the Turkish food his wife had cooked. She was Irish-Australian; however, she could cook Turkish foods well, which İbrahim was very proud of. He thanked her for the meal and sat before the television to watch the evening news, as was his habit. As he watched the ABC News broadcast, one of the news segments in particular grabbed his attention; the military in Turkey had taken over the government once again, just as they had in 1960. They abolished the constitution, and kept many political leaders, including Prime Minister Süleyman Demirel, opposition leader Bülent Ecevit, and the National Salvation Party (MSP) leader Necmettin Erbakan, under house arrest.

İbrahim was disturbed by the news. It was as if the events of the 1960 coup were taking place once again. He knew well what the implications of such an event would be. The Turkey that he loved would regress ten years and fall behind the rest of the world. Turkey's reputation would be damaged once again, and political and economic relations between Turkey and other nations would be strained. The coup would give rise to much corruption and human rights would be trampled. İbrahim did not sleep well that night.

The next morning, İbrahim purchased various newspapers in order to learn more about the coup. Television newscasts provided few details and he was intensely curious about the events occurring in Turkey.

When he had a chance to meet and chat with other Turks, he encountered a sharp division within the Turkish community. The majority of right-wing (and some liberal) Turks were pleased with the coup since the military would decrease the conflicts between extremist political groups in Turkey (i.e., both left- and right-wing political groups). Left-wing Turks opposed the coup, especially because many left-wing politicians, non-government organizations (NGO) leaders, and intellectuals had been arrested.

When İbrahim stated that he too opposed the military coup since it would cripple Turkey, most of the right-wing Turks at the mosque were surprised. They accused him of supporting leftists who were generally antireligious or were agnostic, and included some communists.

İbrahim explained to them that he was thinking about the long-term effects of the coup and the impact it would have on the developing democracy in Turkey. He pointed out that developed countries did not have military rule, and that military rule was predominant in Third World nations. However, he did not take their accusations to heart. In the *Turkish News*, İbrahim did not express support for the coup, even though it was a conservative newspaper.

CONFLICT AND FORMING CYPRIOT TURKISH ISLAMIC SOCIETY (CTIS)

The Dellal brothers, particularly İbrahim, wanted to educate other Cypriots on Islam. This was consistent with the brothers' belief that children should have a solid understanding of their cultural heritage and religion. However, some members of the Cypriot Turkish Society (CTS), especially the secular ones, were not pleased to hear about this goal. There was already some tension between the brothers and the secular Turks since the Dellals began organizing prayer sessions in the building owned by the Cypriot Turkish Society. Indeed, when İbrahim was the president of the CTS in the late 1950s, he would invite Imam Fehmi to lead the Friday prayers at the center in Carlton.

It wasn't until the Preston mosque was purchased that the Friday prayers in Carlton ended.

Some of the secular members of the CTS would organize social events that included the drinking of alcoholic beverages, parties, and minor gambling using the name of the CTS Society to promote such activities and using CTS facilities. The Dellal brothers did not approve of such activities taking place in a building owned by the CTS. Religion was only present in some of the secular members' lives during funeral services and Eids.

The secular-religious tension within the CTS did not help the brothers advance their goal of enhancing the Turks understanding of their heritage and faith. In 1981, the Dellal brothers, together with 20 members of the CTS formed a new and independent organization called the Cypriot Turkish Islamic Society (CTIS). Their aim was to build a mosque, impart moral values to their children, organize religious activities on holy days, and reach out to other Muslims in the area.

In 1986, the CTIS purchased five acres of land in the suburb of Sunshine, Victoria. They placed a portable building as a makeshift mosque on the site and another portable facility to house the imam. The imam arrived in 1988, and in 1991 they laid the foundation of the mosque. Slowly, more Turkish Cypriots began attending the different services offered by the mosque and began to give their support. In return, the CTIS began weekend classes for children. The board members of the CTIS worked on outreach projects through social activities, and increased services to meet the needs of the local Muslim community, especially the Cypriot Turks.

AHMET'S FINAL DAYS

Ahmet Mustafa Dellal, being the oldest of the Dellal brothers, had a significant impact on İbrahim. During İbrahim's first five years in Australia, İbrahim stayed at Ahmet's house. Ahmet was a fatherly figure for İbrahim, while his wife, Iclal, provided İbrahim not only with food, but took care of many of his needs like a traditional mother would. It was Ahmet who helped İbrahim purchase a house. Together, they had established both the Cypriot Turkish Society and Cypriot Turkish Islamic Society.

Ahmet was diagnosed with cancer in 1982 and battled it for three years. İbrahim sadly said, "My brother had many operations at the Royal Melbourne Hospital. The medical technology back then made it difficult, so the doctors had to operate on many parts of his body." When close to death, Ahmet wrote a letter to his wife and daughters, Farial and Fisun. The letter was found after he had passed away. Iclal read the letter once after her husband passed away. It was a painful ordeal for her. She packed the letter away and never read it again. Even İbrahim had not read the letter.

When I visited Iclal with İbrahim, she first showed us pictures of the Dellal brothers. During tea, her husband's name naturally arose, and the conversation flowed from there. She mentioned the letter he left behind. I kindly requested if I could see that letter, not knowing that she had not shown the letter to anyone. Hesitantly, she replied, "Yes" and brought out the five-page letter. She was also generous enough to give me Ahmet's other personal belongings, such as his diary describing the establishment, funding, and outreach activities of the Cypriot Turkish Islamic Society.

In his letter, Ahmet described his final days. On one of the days when his family was with him, he had said to them, "Go now. Pray to God for me." After they left, Ahmet tossed and turned, but could not sleep until late into the night. At 7am, the nurse came to announce that she would perform the necessary preparations for the 8:30 am surgery. Ahmet thought, "After this, I will obey my destiny." He read the opening chapter of the Qur'an once and said the testimony of faith (*shahadah*) three times[60].

---

60 The *shahadah* (testimony of faith) is the first pillar of Islam. It is the creed which outlines the core of Islamic belief: belief in One God and His Messenger, Prophet Muhammad, peace be upon him. It is a tradition to say the *shahadah* at the point of death.

He opened his eyes the next morning after the operation. He believed that his life had permanently changed. Ahmet interpreted this to mean that his life would never be as good as it had been before the surgical procedure. Yet, despite this realization, his religious faith was not shaken. "I thanked God and submitted myself to His will," wrote Ahmet.

The next ten days proved difficult since he was in pain and feverish. The day he was finally able to eat normally, he felt like he was reborn. Even after his discharge, he continued to experience pain. During his home stay, family members, including İbrahim, did not leave his bedside. The compassion shown by his loved ones made him declare that he was grateful to them in both this world and the Hereafter. His letter ended there.

İbrahim recalled:

When I went to visit him, I could not say, *"Gecmis olsun"* (a Turkish idiom meaning "Let it have passed," customarily said to an ill person). I tried to hide the tears as I tried to smile. His voice was almost inaudible, so thin and gentle that I could barely hear him.

My brother asked me, "Do I have to bear this suffering? I know it is my destiny, but there is something that I just cannot work out. Why did you allow them (doctors) to tear me apart so much (with so many operations)?" I replied, "Life is sweet (ie. important). It had to be done. Otherwise, I would feel responsible." There were tears in his eyes as he listened to me. I continued, "I hope you will get well by the grace of God."

Ahmet responded, "I am not afraid of death. When the time comes, it will happen. I am concerned for my children and grandchildren. I wanted to give them a good spiritual upbringing but…" I interrupted his sentence and said to Ahmet, "God willing, you will get better. There are still a lot of things you and I have to do for the community." He replied, "I will not be able to take care of them anymore."

Ahmet was discharged from Royal Melbourne Hospital a week later. He stayed home for a while, but was readmitted due to intense pain. Hearing the news from Iclal, I came by to visit my older brother. My brother, Hasan, Ahmet's wife, Iclal, and daughters were all there. His daughters said their goodbyes and went home. Hasan and Iclal left the room for a while. Ahmet was sitting on his bed and smiling. "You look alright," I said. "Yes," he replied.

His wife and my brother left around midnight, leaving us alone together. He quickly said to me, "Listen to me. Brother, my time has come. My grandchildren are entrusted to you. Please spend time with them and take care of them. Pray for me." I was shocked. I still did not want to believe it. I turned my back to him to shed tears, not wanting to show my pain. When I faced him, I said "No, you and I will do that together. By God's will, you will live on." He looked at me and said, "You can go now." Ahmet's wife and Hasan returned. I left the hospital with Hasan.

Not too long after I left, the news of his death came. When I finally went home, I retreated to my room and cried. I felt like I was crushed under the trust he had given me. I asked for God's help. I gathered myself together. The next day, my brother's body was washed. The funeral prayer was performed in the mosque in Sunshine where it was attended by a large crowd of family and friends. He was buried in Springvale cemetery.

Ahmet had served the community since his arrival in 1948. His funeral service reminded me of Prophet Muhammad's saying, "Seek knowledge from the cradle to the grave." Just like my brother, I too wanted to serve the community until I died. I know that when we make others happy, we become happy.

Ten years had passed since the death of İbrahim's mother, and five years since his father's death. Now İbrahim had to bear another loss. "It was like both my brother and father died at once. But what can you do? It is human destiny," said İbrahim as he struggled to hold back tears when he was telling me about his losses.

FAMILY VISITS

In 1984, İbrahim visited his maternal aunt, Cemaliye, in Mersin, a city in the southern part of Turkey. His grandfather had owned property in Mersin and Iskenderun, both coastal towns located in southern Anatolia. İbrahim's aunt and uncle had moved to Anatolia to manage the family's properties and conduct business.

After the collapse of the Ottoman Empire, the Dellals lost contact with their relatives living in Anatolia. No passenger ships had passed between Mersin and Cyprus since the Turkish Republic had been established. Even postal service was tightly controlled between Turkey and Cyprus. It was possible to send letters through trusted travelers, but it was not until 1948 that a passenger ship departed from Mersin for Cyprus.

Finally, the Dellals in Anatolia were reunited with their relatives in Cyprus for a short time before the relatives had to return to Mersin. Over time, as communication and means of travel between Cyprus and Turkey improved, contact between the Dellals and their Anatolian relatives occurred more frequently.

When İbrahim visited his aunt Cemaliye in 1984, he felt as though he had been reunited with his mother. The elderly aunt spoke at length about what had occurred during her lifetime. İbrahim called her 'a living history' and watched her cry over the stories she told. She was like a mother to İbrahim. He stayed with his aunt for a day and described his life in Australia. İbrahim explained that the opportunities awaiting the settler were a blessing as was the natural beauty of Australia; however, what he loved most about Australia was the opportunity to serve humanity. He stated, "I was helpful to the first migrant Turks and other ethnic migrants such as the Greeks. I would help in translation, finding them homes, jobs, organizing community and religious events, building mosques. This is my hobby and a part of my life that I love. If I do not make these a part of my life, I feel greatly bothered."

That was the last time İbrahim saw his aunt. Her death in 1985 caused İbrahim great sadness. However, İbrahim's belief in the Hereafter remained strong. He knew that life in this world is temporary, and that no one will live forever. He also knew that only the deeds of that person will remain on this planet after the soul has departed.

New Hope

When Turkish immigrants arrived in Australia, their top priority was to build mosques before establishing other institutions and organizations. "Why did they build mosques first?" I asked İbrahim. For

İbrahim, a mosque is a community centre. He said, "It brings people together." A mosque is not only a needed place of worship, but is also an educational facility. Children would learn the basics of religion and the Turkish language in after-school or weekend programs. It served as a youth centre where pride in one's culture was emphasized and it gave the young person a sense of identity and helped them avoid many of the pitfalls associated with Western society such as substance use/abuse.

"Mosques were established to teach people to be good Muslims, law-abiding citizens, loving family members, considerate neighbours, and assets to society through community service," İbrahim stated.

The construction of mosques in Australia also helped to preserve the settlers cultural heritage. Settlers feared "losing" their children in the new land. They worried that their children would forget their religion, Turkish culture, family values, and language. However, the development of Islamic cultural centers and mosques would help settlers educate future generations. That is, children born and raised in Australia would still possess an understanding of their Turkish heritage and religious faith.

The parents wanted their children to maintain family values. For example, due to the sanctity of marriage in Turkish culture, especially before the 1980s, casual relationships, like dating and any premarital relationship were not common and viewed in a negative light. Hence, the social attitudes in Australia would, at times, clash with traditional Turkish values. The parents who intended to return to Turkey one day did not want their children to be unaware of their Turkish roots.

Conversely, some settlers were not concerned about "losing" their children. These settlers were Westernized Turks and had lived in urban settings before they relocated to Australia. Settlers concerned about preserving their cultural heritage tended to be conservative Turks and had resided in rural settings in Turkey before they traveled to Australia.

"Do you think the mosques served their expected purpose?" I asked İbrahim. He replied, "To some extent, yes. However, since there was no capable and qualified educators, only basic religious knowledge was given to the children on part of volunteers, but it was not enough. We needed educated imams who were familiar with Western culture."

When İbrahim learned that the head of the Ministry of Religious Affairs in Turkey, Tayyar Altıkulaç, would visit Australia, he felt that the help Turkish settlers interested in preserving their culture and religious faith needed would finally arrive.

In 1984, Tayyar Altıkulaç visited Sydney and Melbourne, where he met with Turkish Muslim leaders, including İbrahim. Altıkulaç spoke of educating children with moral values in order to prevent them from falling into political Islam or radicalism of any form. During the question-answer session, İbrahim stood up and told Altıkulaç the story of the Cypriot Turks in Australia and how they needed an intelligent imam familiar with both Turkish and Western culture and possessing the skills needed to interact with young people. Altıkulaç promised to send an imam and pay his salary if the different Turkish Islamic societies built a mosque and provided accommodations for the imam.

İbrahim was inspired by Altıkulaç's words and the promise of support. He talked with members of the Cyprus Turkish Islamic Society (CTIS) who were either religious or respectful towards religion. He spoke of the need to build a mosque, especially one close to Sunshine where a substantial number of the CTIS members resided. İbrahim said to the CTIS members who had gathered for a meeting, "The other mosque is too far away. If we wanted to take our children for a weekend class, we would need to travel a long distance. Also, we have some cultural differences that need to be addressed. I think it is time to build a mosque here as Cypriot Turkish Muslims."

In accordance with Altıkulaç's promise, university-educated imams arrived in Australia. The general sentiment in the community was that the "imam and mosque can save my children." This attitude was more prevalent among immigrants who worked long hours and could not spare much time for their children, thus making it harder for their children to be exposed to their cultural heritage. Moreover, parents saw that even if they spoke the same language with their children, they could not understand their children. What the child was taught at home differed from what the child learned at school, on TV, or in the streets. This clash of cultures made parents even more desperate for a solution.

"Did these imams meet the community's expectations?" I asked İbrahim. "Somewhat," İbrahim replied. "The imams could not communicate well with the kids who were raised in Australia. Moreover, the imams had problems communicating in English since it was not their first language." The Ministry of Religious Affairs did send educated imams, but they were not as capable in adapting to the cultural and linguistic differences as the community expected.

At first, there were hundreds of children who would attend the Qur'an classes and weekend programs, but now there aren't as many." "How successful were the weekend programs?" I enquired. İbrahim thought for a minute and said, "If they were very successful, we would not have established schools." When the mosque did not meet all expectations, community members hoped that the development of Islamic schools would satisfy their needs, and offered their support.

According to some of the interviewees who were active on mosque boards and religious organizations, the imams were sent from Turkey to regulate the congregations and decrease the influence of Islamic and Sufi movements. Thus, congregations in Australia would be similar to those in Turkey that were under the control of the secular state. This led to tension between different Muslim groups and the mosque administration. İbrahim felt this too. He said,

> There were times in the Seventies and Eighties when the Turkish consulate in Melbourne urged me not to work for Islamic organizations, and told me that I should focus on secular Turkish organizations alone. I did not want to give a definite answer and bother them, so I would tell them, 'Let me think about it' and leave it at that. Yet I continued to be active in Islamic organizations. As a matter of fact, I had been investigated and reported negatively to the Ministry of Foreign Affairs in Turkey. The Chief of Staff,

General Semih Sancar, was related to me through marriage with my relative in Turkey. When I went to Turkey in 1974, he informed me about the report on me and helped me clean up my record. Apparently, I had been labeled a *"dinci"* (fundamentalist). Fortunately, Turkey has changed in recent years and become more democratic, so consulate staff are respectful towards everyone, despite religious standing.

CHAPTER 9

Hizmet and İbrahim's service

HIZMET AND İBRAHİM'S SERVICE

Hizmet is a key word in the Gülen Movement meaning "service." *Hizmet* firstly means "service to others". *Hizmet* refers to various activities organised by the Gülen Movement towards educational, charitable, religious, interfaith, and nondenominational realisations, including non-religious secular deeds. The Gülen Movement is named by Western intellectuals after Fethullah Gülen[61], a renown Muslim scholar who is the source of inspiration for the participants of this movement to open schools all over the world and engage with all human beings with compassion, love, and understanding. Gülen is also known as a contemporary Rumi (1207–1273).

Gülen began as a small town preacher in Turkey who was inspired by Jalal ad-Din Rumi, Muhammad Lutfi Efendi (1868–1956), and Said Nursi (1877–1960). He classified the enemies of Islam into three: ignorance, poverty, and disunity. Without education, ignorance will be rampant, and poverty will be widespread. His ideas revolved around solving community problems through moral education. His dream was to rid Turkey of its spiritual and social ills. To fulfill his aims, he used all of his time, financial resources, and social connections. His devotion to improving the community is the spirit of *Hizmet*, the Turkish name for the Gülen Movement. Bearing an influential power like Ghandi, Gülen chose non-violent activism and soon garnered the interests of others.

---

61 Erkan Toguslu, "*Hizmet*: from *Futuwwa* tradition to the emergence of movement in public space." Georgetown University Conference Proceedings of "Islam in the age of global challenges: Alternative perspectives of the Gülen Movement" p.711-727

The Gülen Movement started with a group of individuals under the spiritual leadership of Fethullah Gülen in Izmir, Turkey. The movement is dedicated to helping humanity through quality education and community service. Today, the movement has millions of followers globally. It has led to the establishment of thousands of educational institutions and cultural organizations. The educational institutions range from childcare centres to universities, while cultural organizations include media groups, interfaith dialogue foundations, and charitable institutions.

Gülen discussed his ideas to whoever would listen to him at mosques, coffee houses and universities. His ideas impressed many youth and businessmen. He encouraged those who followed his ideas to open dorms where at-risk youth could receive a moral, spiritual, and secular education and be filled with the spirit of serving one's community. The first dorm was opened in the 1970s. With the support of dedicated friends and kindred hearts, the small group then moved onto opening a school where the "Golden Generation" would be educated. The "Golden Generation" as envisioned by Gülen are youth who are educated with moral values and dedicated to serve humanity.

In time, more schools opened. A need for university preparation centres grew, so those were established as well throughout Turkey. Through the encouragement of Gülen, his followers voluntarily migrated to Central Asia, which had just come out from the collapse of Communism, and established educational institutions there. As years went by, thousands of educational and cultural centres opened in more than a hundred countries, including Australia.

His followers come from all branches of life and spheres of professions. Recognising the potential of his followers, Gülen encouraged them to establish non-government organisations, such as charity organisations, women's groups, businesses, media outlets, publishing houses, cultural centres, and interfaith dialogue centres[62].

---

62 Marcia Hermansen, The Cultivation of Memory in the Gülen Community, Leeds Metropolitan University Press International Conference Proceedings of Muslim World in Transition: Contribution of the Gülen Movement, p.60-75.

The Gülen Movement spread to Australia with the initiative of Orhan Çiçek who arrived as a migrant in 1981. Together with others who followed Gülen's philosophy, Orhan Çiçek established The New Generation Youth Association based in the Melbourne suburbs of Richmond, Sunshine, Broadmeadows, and Dandenong. Two years later, they formed the Light Tutoring Centre, a free tuition centre aimed at Muslim students. In 1991, Orhan met with İbrahim at a mosque. They continue their relationship after their meeting. In the same year, Orhan, İbrahim, and others establish the Selimiye Foundation, aiming to open private schools in Australia. A sister organisation, Feza Foundation, was founded in Sydney in 1993. In 1996, the first Gülen-inspired school in Australia opened in Prestons, Sydney and was named Sule College. In 1997, Işık College opened in Eastmeadows, Melbourne. Today, there are 14 schools and school campuses in NSW, Victoria, Adelaide, Brisbane, and Perth[63].

Becoming a Volunteer in the Gülen Movement

In 1989, İbrahim met Orhan Çiçek. Orhan immigrated to Melbourne in 1982. He was a teacher in Turkey, and came to Australia to marry a Turkish. He worked at blue-collar jobs, but his passion was helping the Turkish and Muslim communities, particularly the youth. He was one of the few Turkish teachers that İbrahim met who practiced his religion. He was not only practicing, but was active in educating others about religion through religious study circle. Orhan invited İbrahim to attend a weekly study circle place at the Coburg Mosque.

That day, Mehmet Ali Şengül, a student of Fethullah Gülen, a global spiritual leader, was leading the religious study circle. Mehmet Ali spoke about approaching humans with love and compassion.

---

[63] Greg Barton, How the Hizmet works: Islam, dialogue, and the Gülen movement in Australia, p.114-137, Georgetown University Conference Proceedings of "Islam in the age of global challenges: Alternative perspectives of the Gülen Movement" p.711-727

Mehmet Ali seemed to speak directly to İbrahim, who thought, "For years, this is exactly what I had been looking for." After the religious study circle was over, Orhan invited İbrahim to attend another weekly religious study circle. Orhan was someone who had been inspired by Fethullah Gülen's vision and philisophy. Through these study circles, İbrahim was introduced to the *Hizmet*, also known as the Gülen Movement. *Hizmet* means "service." Indeed, to serve one's family and country is a primary value in Turkish Muslim culture.

Baki Tanrıverdi immigrated in 1972 and established the Turkish Islamic Society in Mildura. He is also a close friend of Dellal and has great respect for him. Baki stated:

> İbrahim is a well disciplined, caring, exceptionally friendly, and kind person. He does not lose hope quickly in difficult times. He is an Ottoman *beyefendisi* (sir)[64] and a very gentle and encouraging person dedicated to serve humanity. İbrahim is great person however he is not arrogant but is humble. I think İbrahim is one of the most trusted persons in our community. Australian officials trust him too. He is man of rules and a law-abiding citizen. He never wants to break any rules or conventions. He is a hard worker. Sometimes he works seven days a week voluntarily. About two years ago he had heart attack while he was working voluntarily on a Sunday. Despite his sickness, he did not want go home without finishing the work. If there is ever a thing needed for the community or by the community, Dellal would work night and day until its execution. He helps everyone without any expectation or reward in return.

İbrahim, Orhan Çiçek, Mehmet Aydınoğlu, Dr. Gürsel Alpay, Tayfun Eren, Tuncay Terzi, Harun Yüksel, Ahmet Veli, Vahit Güler, and Ekrem Cebeci founded the Selimiye Foundation, a non-profit organization aiming to educate the Turkish Muslim community through educational institutions and community activities. İbrahim served as a board member since 1991 as the foundation's president since 1994. Besides the men mentioned, there were more than a hun-

---

64   A polite honorific term used after a man's first name in Turkish language/culture.

dred volunteers in the beginning, and this number grew with time. They were involved in every aspect, from construction work and financial support to spreading the word and providing seminars at the Foundation. Some of the volunteers did not want to be mentioned.

The first initiative of the Selimiye Foundation was to open a dormitory for high school students in Dallas, Victoria and run it until they were financially able to establish a school. They began with 20 male students. Their aim was to provide quality education and spiritual guidance for Turkish youth who were at risk of losing their cultural heritage. After the foundation opened the dormitory, they decided to establish a new school. After much thought and research, İbrahim, Orhan, and their circle of friends at the foundation established a school designed to satisfy the needs of Turkish-Australian children.

Orhan Çiçek's Reflections on İbrahim Dellal

I met İbrahim Dellal a few times before I invited him to our dershane (student dormitory) at Richmond to join the religious discussions. I knew that he had worked hard to establish mosques and help the community. He was alienated by some Muslims because of some of his views. For example, although he worked hard to establish Coburg Mosque, some Muslims were not happy to see him there.

İbrahim is an Ottoman Beyefendi as well as an English Sir. He brought Ottoman tradition and English tradition together. He uses the best of both traditions to present himself like a diplomat, using the right words to build bridges and make connections every day.

He did not receive respect from some religious Turks and non-Turkish Muslims, probably because of his pro-Atatürk view. However, Hizmet (members of the Gülen Movement) did not alienate him because of his views. He loved Mehmet Ali Şengül's talk at Coburg Mosque, especially Şengül's words, "We are lovers of love and we have no time for animosity."

When İbrahim came to the dershane[65] for a visit, there were about 20 people present at the time and all of them showed great respect towards him. The young kissed his hand which is a sign of respect towards the elders and the elders hugged him with affection. İbrahim was moved by the welcome he received.

With time, he read Fethullah Gülen's articles, books and started learning more about Hizmet. He was greatly influenced by Gülen's approach to serving humanity through love and compassion. He learned a lot from Hizmet's philosophy and he digested what he learnt very well.

İbrahim played an important role in organising Muslims, establishing the Islamic Society of Victoria, the Australian Federation of Islamic Council (AFIC) and establishing mosques. Whenever and wherever there was a community activity or Islamic activity, İbrahim tried to be there and tried his best to help. From that point of view, he is a unique person.

To me, the best thing he did was to sell Australian meat to Muslim countries such as Saudi Arabia, Iran and the Gulf States. He travelled with Dr. Kazi to Saudi Arabia, Iran and other Muslim countries to discuss the purchasing of halal meat from Australia. He organised and persuaded government officials in Muslim countries to purchase halal meat from businesses in Australia. Since then, Australia has sold halal meat and made billions of dollars. A small percentage of that money has been given to the Muslim community in Australia to build mosques and educational institutions.

İbrahim also led the Muslim community in Australia in sending their Qurban meat[66] overseas as humanitarian aid. In 1992, Qurban was collected for Bosnian victims of war. İbrahim used his connections to send the

---

65   Dershane literally means "place of study." It is a small dorm that functions according to basic principles of the Gülen Movement. There are ground rules, such as curfew and chores, which are agreed upon by all dorm residents. An older student who is morally and educationally exemplary manages the dershane daily. The dershane managers are called "abi" (older brother) or "abla" (older sister), and are noted for their dedication to education and Hizmet.

66   Qurban meat is the meat of the animal (usually lamb) which is sacrificed during the "Festival of Sacrifice" (Eidul Adha). It is a symbolic act which traces back to the story of Prophet Abraham's sacrifice. It is also an opportunity to donate to the poor. For many poor communities, this is the only time they get to eat meat.

meat *of Qurban to Bosnia through Merhamet (Bosnian Red Crescent) for humanitarian aid. This became an example for other Muslims who also started sending their Qurban meat overseas to needy people. With time, this became a tradition for Muslims in Europe and the Muslim world, especially Turkish Muslims.*

A few radical left-wing Turks, whom I do not want to name, published news in the weekly Turkish Report, *a locally published Turkish newspaper, indicating that İbrahim Dellal and I used the Qurban money for our own benefit. The newspaper was sued, but because the case took a long time, we did not have enough money to pay for a lawyer. İbrahim defended the case as a lawyer and we finally won the case. I was amazed at İbrahim's defense. The judge decided that the defendant would have to pay $21,000 to İbrahim and $11,000 to me. İbrahim said about the money that needed to be paid, "Those who wrote false news about us do not own anything like a house or business. They can not pay this. Together with the interest accrued on the due amount, it may be over $70,000. I have no intention of following up with this case. I leave them to God*[67]*."*

When there was no media communication between Turkey and Australia, İbrahim published Turk Sesi *a Turkish weekly newspaper. He wrote the English version of the newspaper, but labeled it* Turkish News *instead of the exact translation of "Turkish Voice" because the former sounded more like a newspaper. He would listen to short radio waves and write the news about Turkey. Such news would help Turkish immigrants morally. Until we were able to receive the Turkish daily* Zaman *newspaper in Melbourne, he would use it as a news source for the* Turkish News. Turkish News *later became weekly* Zaman Australia.

İbrahim does not act like a retired man. He still shaves daily, puts on his suit and tie, and then steps out of his home.

---

67 In Muslim culture, it is tradition to forgive those who committed injustices. The phrase "leave it to God" means that a person will not seek revenge or compensation against the unjust party, so instead the judgment is left up to God to either forgive or punish in either this world or the Hereafter.

He is a man of his word. I admire his optimism, determination, discipline and his trust in God. After he became active in the Gülen Movement, he became more determined and optimistic.

İBRAHİM DELLAL MEETS WITH FETHULLAH GÜLEN

After İbrahim encountered the Gülen Movement, he began to listen to the lectures and sermons of the movement's spiritual leader, Fethullah Gülen. Soon İbrahim was reading books and articles authored by Gülen provided by Orhan Çiçek and Mehmet Ali Şengül. Both Orhan and Mehmet Ali had embraced Gülen's ideals.

İbrahim loved Gülen's interpretation of Islam, his simple lifestyle, and his principle of performing every act with compassion. İbrahim felt that he had found exactly what he was looking for. He wanted to meet with Gülen and see for himself the man who spoke of love of God and humanity.

İbrahim's chance came in 1991 when the University of Adelaide sponsored a research project involving livestock. Through genetic manipulation, researchers at the university were able to induce the animals to give birth more than once a year. This procedure would be of great value to livestock farmers. When İbrahim heard of this research, he thought that it would be very useful for the livestock industry in Turkey and suggested to the researchers that they sell their procedure to Turkish businesspersons. The researchers took İbrahim's advice and asked if İbrahim would serve as an interpreter and guide for their business trip to Turkey.

When Orhan heard that İbrahim was heading to Turkey, he suggested that he meet with Gülen. İbrahim agreed without hesitation. Orhan arranged for İbrahim to meet with Gülen in Çamlıca, Istanbul. İbrahim and Gülen had breakfast together. Gülen asked İbrahim to sit beside him in a dining hall where others who came to see Gülen were also present. İbrahim was captivated by the spiritual atmosphere that surrounded Gülen and those who came to see him.

İbrahim fondly remembers their short conversation. He recalled telling Gülen that "the Australian Muslim community is in need of Muslims who represent Islam with love and without politicizing Islam." Gülen placed his hand on İbrahim's knee and said, "You will do more beneficial services for the community by God's will." Gülen then said something that İbrahim would repeat in many of his speeches and personal talks. Gülen said, "Life is too short. There is much important work to be done. We have no time for quarrelling." İbrahim left Gülen's presence feeling inspired with a greater desire to serve.

In 1992, İbrahim heard from Orhan that Gülen would be coming to Australia to lay the foundation of the first dormitory at 21 Lismore St, Dallas, Victoria, and that he would remain in Australia for a few more days to attend a retreat. İbrahim eagerly awaited Gülen's arrival in June. According to the program, İbrahim would be with Gülen at the laying of the foundation and then at the retreat.

In Australia, Gülen spoke about *muhabbet* (love) as it is related to a person's relationship with God and other human beings. He stressed positive thinking and action without discrimination. He also focused on education, especially on the power of combining the education of mind and heart. His ideal educational centre would teach its students how to be more compassionate beings alongside learning about the arts and sciences.

Gülen had witnessed the establishment and success of schools that focused on educating both the mind and heart in Turkey and Central Asia, and saw the same spirit for service in the hearts of the retreat attendees. He said, "The schools that you will establish will be successful in education and contribute to Australia, but you will go through many hardships to achieve this. However, do not despair." Gülen realized that it would be a first for the Turkish community in Australia. The community's inexperience combined with weak financial resources would make the process of establishing schools more difficult.

İbrahim recalled, "The days I spent with *Hoca Efendi*[68] (Gülen) were the greatest days in my life." "*Hoca Efendi* would speak briefly and essentially. He would worship during the night. He would speak about love and compassion often." The few days İbrahim spent with Gülen were not enough. "We wanted to be with Gülen longer. The retreat was memorable both physically and spiritually."

First School

The Selimiye Foundation began to search for available plots of land and houses to open the school. The Foundation had little money, a few thousand dollars at most according to İbrahim. However, they were optimistic about the support of the community since they had received support when they opened the dormitory. At the fundraising dinner for the dormitory project, there were approximately 50-60 individuals who either directly contributed or pledged over $70,000. Moreover, members of the Foundation and the community devoted their time and skills to preparing the dormitory building. Thus, İbrahim and the board members were full of hope that they would successfully establish a new school.

Through the Ministry of Education, they learned that several school buildings were for sale in Eastmeadows, a suburb with the greatest number of Turkish and Muslim families in Victoria. At that time, the campus had a few portable buildings and vacant land. After inspecting the school grounds and considering the prices, they agreed to pay a $50,000 down payment. Before the contract that covered the payment details was even signed, İbrahim gave $20 that was in his pocket to show the Foundation's immense desire to start the process.

After a few days, the board members went to the Ministry of Education to sign the final contract. After signing, they waited to receive the keys and security code. Unfortunately, they were to be disappoint-

---

68 Hoca (pronounced hodja) is the Turkish word for teachers of all levels, imam, or spiritual leaders. Efendi is an Ottoman term meaning "sir." Those in the Gülen Movement refer to Gülen as Hoca Efendi.

ed. A bureacrat approached them, and informed them that although there was an agreement, the head of the Board of Education refused to sell the school because the correct procedures had not been followed. He stated that the building must first be advertised in the newspaper, and then it must be auctioned off to the highest bidder. Interestingly, other schools had been sold without proper advertising. İbrahim believed that someone in the Turkish community had complained to the Board of Education out of personal anger towards the Foundation since he had several experiences with individuals who opposed the Foundation's activities.

The Foundation's board members were persistent. They waited for hours at the office, stating that they could not turn back after all their hard work of collecting funds and persuading the community to support the new school. It was ridiculous to have agreed on a deposit, signed the agreement, and given a down payment for the building only to learn that they could not complete the transaction at the last moment. Moreover, some families had already submitted their enrollment applications for their children.

The administrator in the office struggled to process their request and allow the purchase to go through. However, after hours of waiting, the administrator stated that there was a definite order from the head of the Board of Education not to sell the school to the Selimiye Foundation. "At that moment, it felt as though all my hopes had washed away," İbrahim remarked.

Weary from the hours of waiting, the board members made their way to their parked car. One member asked, "İbrahim *abi*[69], what are we going to do?" İbrahim turned to the man and said, "Do not worry. This is not over yet." Within a week, the members spoke with the local ruling and opposition parties about this issue. News came that the board members were to have a meeting at the Board of Education's office again.

---

[69] In Turkish culture, elders are not called by their names directly. Out of respect, males who are at least a few years older are called *abi* (big brother) while females are called *abla* (big sister). This applies to both families and non-related persons.

The board members were hopeful and glad to have İbrahim by their side. They knew that he could speak English well and earned respect since he had received a Silver Jubilee Medal. They were accompanied by Ali Riza Gurcanli, who would serve as the school's principal, and the Foundation's accountant, Mehmet Aydinoglu. İbrahim would speak for the group since his English was fluent.

A committee of five had gathered to listen to the Foundation's proposal. İbrahim put forward the following arguments:

> In our community, there are third-class citizens in great need of education. They cannot provide proper education for themselves or their children. The local government knows about our educational activities. Nick Bulkos, Federal Immigration Minister, attended the opening of our dormitory. Moreover, we were promised this school, so we even accepted nearly thirty early enrolments within that week. I cannot give such bad news to this community. I would never be able to do that. This community relies on us. What can we tell them? The community members pledged financial support for our school. Some even gave us cash on the spot. If we cannot purchase this school building, it will be a terrible blow to our Foundation's reputation and it will have a massive financial impact on us.

The committee members began asking questions. They asked for written documents indicating the pledge amounts made by community members. The Foundation's accountant provided the necessary paperwork. After inspecting the stack of pledge papers, the committee was convinced. The head of the committee rose and said, "This school is now yours. You promised the people, accepted money, and gave them hope. So we have to give you this school." The Foundation's accountant provided the full deposit, signed the agreement, and received the keys of the school.

In spite of the feeling of relief that came with receiving the keys, the board members were still anxious. The unnecessary delay had wasted valuable time that they needed to prepare the school for the upcoming semester. However, they did not intend to push back the opening date. İbrahim said to the committee, "We will open this school in three days. We invite you all to our opening." The committee was shocked. İbrahim could tell by the looks on their faces that they did not believe him. The school was in desperate need of renovations that would take at least three months to complete, let alone three days. Yet the board members were so happy that they finally had purchased a school building that they did not fear the daunting task ahead of him.

The board members quickly gathered their families and friends, forming a 60-person team, and spent the next 78 hours working on the school. They painted the walls, replaced the windows, purchased new carpets and tables, cleaned the halls, and checked the plumbing and electricity. They did not sleep much since their time was short.

On Monday, İbrahim again visited the Ministry of Education to obtain the final consent for the opening of the school and to inform that the school would be ready for opening. The property unit manager was surprised and said, "It's impossible. It's a three-month job minimum to renovate that building. You cannot finish in three days. Did you repair the broken glass windows? There's more than 150."

İbrahim replied, "Yes."

"Did you fix the broken doors?"

İbrahim again replied, "Yes."

"What about painting all the walls?"

İbrahim smiled and said, "That's done too."

The manager's eyes widened at each affirmative answer. He asked, "How about the carpets? Did you change those?"

"Yes, we have," İbrahim calmly replied.

"What about the outside of the building? The grounds? Did you clear those?"

"Yes."

"Don't tell me that you have already purchased the tables, chairs, and cabinets too?"

İbrahim chuckled. "Oh, we have taken care of that as well."

It was too much for the manager. "It's impossible. How can you do this? It's impossible." He expected that the Selimiye Foundation would work through the usual process of advertising for a contractor, working out a contract for hours, raising funds for the building, and pass decisions through board meetings as they come up, which would have taken at least three months. When he saw İbrahim's confidence, he said, "The speed of your work is not something humans can do. Is there anyone who helped you?"

İbrahim proudly said, "Yes, there were others."

The manager asked, "Who helped you?"

İbrahim replied, "The angels."

The manager was shocked. "Are you serious?"

İbrahim answered, "Well, you said yourself that humans cannot do this."

The manager said, "You remind me of the early Turks (the Ottomans)."

İbrahim prodded him further. "What do you mean by that?"

The manager told him, "Our grandparents used to say, 'If the Ottomans said they would do something, they would make sure they did it.' You said that you would do one thing and you did two things. Congratulations. I see that you have surpassed them."

The local leading and opposition party members were invited to the opening. The school opened on the 17th of February 1997 with two administrators, Ali Rıza Gürcanlı and assistant principal Tülin Ergi, two teachers, and 28 students. It was called Işık College, with *Işık* meaning "light" in Turkish. The founders intended to educate "the Golden Generation," a generation devoted to service to humanity. İbrahim noted:

> For the first two years, even though I had no telephone in my office, I did whatever job was needed by the Selimiye Foundation or school. In the first year, we had a hard time meeting the teachers' salaries. The principal, Ali Rıza Gürcanlı, was receiving less than half his deserved salary. The cleaning and construction jobs were done voluntarily by board members. We did not even have the

money to purchase stationery. Mehmet Aydinoglu was one of the hardest working among the board members. I asked him to find funds for us, and he obtained a $1,000 loan in response to the request. Other necessities were also purchased using loans.

Together with those I already mentioned, like the board members, there were hundreds of unrecognised heroes who devoted their time, money, and prayers to making our dream a reality. Each one has laid a brick either physically, financially, or spiritually in our school. I can not forget them.

By the end of the first year 64 students were attending the school. During that first year only elementary school-age students (grades prep – 5th) attended. During the second year, there was a dramatic increase in the number of students. 286 children attended the school and grade levels 6th through 8th were added. During the third year, the number of students attending the school increased to 460. Portable buildings were used to accommodate the students.

When I asked Ibrahim for the secret to such a sharp increase in student numbers, Ibrahim smiled and said with confidence, "It was everyone working in the school, from the principal to the janitor, and the volunteers. They worked day and night. There were some of the teachers who not only worked during regular hours, but sincerely volunteered just as much after hours and weekends. That is the secret to the school's success. If you try to ask these heroes to give their names for this book, they will prefer not to."

DANDENONG CAMPUS OPENING

Işık College began to attract Turks from all over suburbs surrounding Melbourne. Starting from 1998, some Turkish parents residing in Dandenong, a suburb located southeast of Melbourne, enrolled their children in Işık College and faced the 60km drive during peak hour. It was, of course, a difficult commute for the children. Parents from Dandenong would often ask Selimiye Foundation's board members, "Why don't you build a branch here in Dandenong as well? There is great need here too."

Objections were raised on the grounds that the Selimiye Foundation did not have the necessary funds. Despite objections, a committee was formed to search for potential school grounds or school buildings. For months, the issue of establishing a new campus was greatly debated at board meetings. There were financial concerns as well as fears that they would not be able to enrol a sufficient number of students or attract experienced teachers.

The committee learned that 10 acres of farmland were available in Keysborough, a suburb of the City of Greater Dandenong; however, there were several concerns. First, the land was worth half a million dollars, far beyond what the Selimiye Foundation had planned on spending. Second, the farmland did not seem to be particularly attractive. Moreover, it was zoned for use as farmland, and the Selimiye Foundation would have to file an application with the local council for a zoning change.

Kemal Şahin, who served as an advisor to the Selimiye Foundation, persuaded the board to move forward with the purchase and convinced them that the aforementioned obstacles could be overcome. "I trusted the Turkish community in Dandenong. I believed they would support us," said Kemal. İbrahim realized that Kemal's words had touched the hearts of supporters. İbrahim reminded the board members that their main objective was to offer Turkish children a quality education and instill moral values. Thus, their goal was to ensure that Turkish children become good citizens of Australia. He informed the board members that he would address the legal issues (i.e., obtaining consent from the town council).

With the aid of Selimiye coordinator Talha Turgut, Dandeong Selimiye board members, and members of the Turkish community in Dandenong, the Foundation held several fundraisers and auctions. Individuals supporting the school raised money through garage sales and bake sales. The Foundation applied for loans from the bank and government grants. After two years, the Turkish community had raised enough money to purchase the land, but continued fundraising activities to make the remaining payments.

There was still the issue of the zoning change. İbrahim went many times to the mayor's office with Ömer Attila Ergi, another board member of the Foundation. They met with the relevant bureaucrats, but were unable to resolve the zoning problem. They later learned that real estate entrepreneurs wanted modify the zoning status so that they could construct residential units. After many visits to the office and countless meetings, İbrahim and Omer finally persuaded the council to change the zoning status. İbrahim recalled, "We were fortunate. The area around the school grounds was changed from farm to residential areas."

Once the change in zoning status was approved, the local Turks provided much needed support. First, they focused all efforts on raising funds. The land was purchased, but there were no buildings, furniture, or supplies. The board members decided not to wait for funds to construct new buildings, and chose to purchase portable buildings. Community members helped clean buildings, assisted with landscaping, installed necessary electricity and plumbing, provided food for the workers, and located families who would be interested in enrolling their children. In fact, most of this work was completed by volunteers. İbrahim said, "I was amazed at the collective work. Everyone was working so hard throughout the day. Some came after the long work hours to help, while others worked overnight and on weekends." Among those hardworking souls Ibrahim mentioned were Yavuz Aşik, the first principal of Dandenong campus, board member Hadi Kırmacı, Osman Balkaya, Necati Eskin, Şevki and Mehmet Yaydemir, Sedat Coşkundağ, Aytekin Şimşek, Cengiz Kaya, and many others.

In January 2001, Işık College Dandenong campus opened with 30 students attending, two teachers, and one principal.

Initially, elementary school-age children attended Işık College. In 2008, the school had its first graduates, and among them were students who had been attending the school since it first opened. 18 of the 20 graduates had been accepted into universities around Victoria. At the first graduation ceremony, İbrahim saw 20 students proudly standing before their parents, and could not help but shed tears at a dream that had come true. "I am the happiest man in the world," he thought. He glanced at the community leaders, parents, and friends who were also at the ceremony and saw the happiness in their eyes. "Everyone knew how difficult it was to open this school, and experienced the pains and joys throughout the years together. Looking at these students made everyone proud," he said.

ARSON

On November 11, 2004, the Eastmeadows campus hosted an *iftar* dinner (the fast-breaking meal during the month of Ramadan) for parents and students. İbrahim and the board members attended this *iftar*, talked with parents, and received feedback. İbrahim felt pleased to hear that the students' parents were satisfied.

That night, as individuals were leaving the dinner, they came across a few men sitting by the curb across the school. The men had been drinking and they offended a few parents with rude behaviour and inappropriate speech. Parents called the principal, Erdal Koçak, and informed him of the matter. The principal said that it was best to leave the men alone since they may not be fully aware of their actions when drunk. One of the men lived near the school. The principal preferred to speak with the man the next morning and did not contact the police.

According to the principal, this was the first time that the neighbor had exhibited such behavior. The principal explained:

> The neighbour had applied to work as a crossing guard by the school (helping the students cross the busy road after school) and had been working for one year. Once, there was a problem in his kitchen. We sent our school's handyman to do some repairs as an act of kindness. He had also been invited to lunch at school several times. Hours after the *iftar*, I received a call from his neighbours whom our school had a good relations with. They would sometimes volunteer at our school. They told me that one of the school buildings was on fire. I immediately called the fire department and came to the school. It was around 1:30am. The police were already there and had set up a barricade.

The police asked me if our school community had anyone who would incite hatred. I told them about the vandalism incident we had, but that was it. Vandals had sprayed offensive graffiti, like the word "pigs" and "dogs", on the school yard. I added that there were some drunk men nearby that night. The neighbours said that the drunk men were around most of the night acting strange and if they did not commit the crime themselves, they may have seen something. Of course, that night, we called İbrahim *abi*.

İbrahim woke up wondering who would call at such a late hour. Still drowsy from sleep, he picked up the telephone hoping it was nothing serious. "When I received the bitter news, I was dumbfounded," said İbrahim. "I washed my face, made ablution, and left for the school. I jumped into my car and arrived, but I was worried all the way there. When I saw the school, I thought, 'It's nearly the end of the year. There are VCE[70] and school exams going on. What are we going to do? We need to find a quick solution.' On one hand, I was worrying about the students, on the other hand, I had hope that God would help us." Optimism and hopefulness were intrinsic to İbrahim's character.

During the confusion, İbrahim and the other Muslims did not forget what also needed to be done. İbrahim recalled, "Since it was Ramadan, we needed to have our *sahur* meal before dawn to prepare for the fast. One of my friends was considerate enough to bring some food and we ate there."

ABC (Australian Broadcasting Company) News reporters were already on site when İbrahim arrived. By morning, most of the major news outlets had sent reporters and camera crews. Both Mr. Koçak and İbrahim gave short statements. İbrahim said, "We let them know that we held no grudges nor had issues with anyone, and that we did not blame anyone for what happened."

---

[70] VCE stands for Victorian Certificate of Education. It is the credential awarded to students who have successfully completed high school subjects. They are taken in the last two years of high school, and are significant when determining university placements.

Within 18 hours, the police had identified the perpetrator. It was the crossing guard. He started the arson by filling a beer bottle with petrol and throwing it at the school. Ironically, the crossing guard was also the first to call the fire department when the blaze began to spread. "The fact that the crossing guard had acted alone was a relief to me. When we informed the parents that the perpetrator was a single man and not an organised hate group, they felt relieved as well and had some peace when sending their children to school," İbrahim said.

Community members were shocked, especially since the crime had occurred during the holy month of Ramadan. The school administration decided to give the 750 students attending the school (from prep-Year 12) a week off so that police and fire investigators could inspect the school and workers could clean the area. The school needed that time to repair the building. Metropolitan Fire Brigade Commander, Ian Yates, reported that the estimated damage from the blaze was $200,000 to $600,000 ("School Blaze Follows Racist Taunts," *The Age*[71], Andrea Petrie, 12 Nov 2004).

The financial damage could be estimated, but the psychological damage was hard to measure. It came as a great surprise that an arsonist would target a school. The fire burned the work that students had produced throughout the year and many school supplies. Furthermore, the fire occurred during one of the busiest times in the school year. Some parents were afraid to send their children back to school and worried about the impact that the fire would have on their children. Moreover, they feared for their children's safety.

İbrahim was greatly saddened. Four classrooms had been completely destroyed, while others had been partially damaged by the fire. İbrahim said:

> The first day was very hard. Together with the administration, we thought about where we could place the students whose classrooms had burned down. Once the Melbourne community

---

71   The Age newspaper is one the broadsheet daily newspapers with the greatest circulation.

received the news, they immediately contacted us, expressing their sympathy and extending their help. I cannot forget the help we received. Our local member of Parliament, John Bromby (current Premier), visited the school. I had called him on Friday and left a message. He came the next day. He connected us with Lynne Kosy, State Education Minister. They offered us a rental school building in Upfield (4km from Eastmeadows campus), which is currently the secondary boys' campus. It was going to be closed down at the end of that year. The fire occurred on Friday morning, and we were granted the temporary campus by 11am on Monday. The news was a great relief to us all. Some of us even shed tears of happiness. I thought, "All praise be to God. A door was closed, but God opened another." The members of the community did not hesitate to express their appreciation to the local government.

We also had NGOs call us and some even visited us. Among the NGOs were church groups and Jewish organizations. Different representatives from local schools and Muslim organizations also came.

The support shown by the community inspired both the school administration and its supporters to gather together as a symbol of solidarity. Within one month of the fire, the school held an interfaith program with 250 attendees.

The Age reported that Michael Lipshutz, president of the Jewish Community Council of Victoria, condemned those who were responsible. He stated, "No matter what political differences may exist in our broader Australian society, there is no place for racism of any kind, whether it be directed against the Muslim community, Jewish community or any other community group."

By 16th of December, Işık College received the keys to the Upfield buildings. Fortunately, the VCE students were finished with their exams and were no longer using their classrooms. İbrahim noted "We shifted the classrooms around. The other students whose classrooms burned down had classes in the library and recreation room. The local mayor offered space at the local learning centre, but it was not practical, so the principal offered his thanks and kindly rejected."

The administration did not want to lose any additional time and further disrupt the students' academic pursuits. Once they received the keys for the Upfield campus, they immediately requested help from the school and the wider community to prepare the new grounds. Students and their parents (and other relatives) as well as neighbours and others volunteered to help.

They divided the tasks. Some cleaned the school grounds. Others painted the classrooms. Some fixed broken doors and windows. Those who could not come to help at the school cooked food for the volunteers and workers. The campus was ready within a week. The mayor and councillors quickly processed the request for the certification of occupation.

IŞIK COLLEGE: A RESOUNDING SUCCESS

Işık College's achievements reflected well on the Selimiye Foundation's goal of providing Turkish students with a quality education. According to school reports, a substantial number of graduates (70% class of 2002) went on to attend university. In 2003, an even greater number of graduates (80%) pursued a university education.

In 2004, the Victorian Government's "On Track Survey Data" ranked Işık College as the second best school in Victoria due to university enrolments, with a truly remarkable number of graduates (94%) going on to enroll in a university. In 2005, it was listed as the top school in the Northern suburbs, and was ranked second in Victoria with the entire class of 2005 going on to attend university. In 2006, news of the school's first place ranking (university enrolments) appeared in *The Age* and *The Herald*.

Eastmeadow's girls campus was ranked first (100% university enrollment), while the Upfield Boys campus ranked third (95% enrollment). In 2007, the entire graduating class on the girls campus went on to attend university and was ranked number one by the government's "On Track Survey," while the Upfield Boys campus reported 98% university enrollment. Rankings appeared in *The Age* and *The Herald* and on June 16, 2008. While rankings are not the only indicator of the school's success in relation with its goals, it nonetheless pleased İbrahim to see that Turkish youth were receiving higher education.

The college's success becomes even more notable when evaluated in light of its environment. VCE Coordinator Mehmet Koca said, "The school is located in the northern suburbs where the unemployment rate and migrant population is very high. These have negative effects on students' success, especially if the language spoken at home is not English. We tried to overcome these difficulties by establishing a close relationship with students and their families. If you can show students that you believe in them, they tend to reflect this is in their attitude towards their studies."

The success of Işık College came to the attention of the Governor of Victoria, Professor David de Krester. He visited the school several times. He congratulated the school community for their successes and contributions to the education of the children of Australia. İbrahim accompanied the Governor during each of his visits. İbrahim noted, "He encouraged us to continue on this path. Each time he visited us, he came into the classrooms and spoke with the students. I thanked him on behalf of the school community for the opportunities the Australian local and federal government secured for our school. He is a humble man. I truly respect him."

Hasan Dellal's Passing

Hasan Dellal graduated from the American Academy in Larnaca and then he immigrated to Australia in 1948. He landed a job at an Australian post office and worked for the postal service for almost eleven years. In 1954 he was the first Turk to attend a memorial service at Canberra's Anzac War Memorial where he placed a garland on the memorial on behalf of the Turkish Community in Australia. He had obtained permission from the Turkish Prime Minister Adnan Menderes to place the garland on the war memorial. Hasan also worked with his brother İbrahim to help Turkish settlers adapt to their new homeland.

Hasan passed away on July 31, 2000, before the Sunshine mosque had officially opened. Before he died, he told İbrahim, "My greatest goal was to finish the construction of the Turkish Cypriot mosque, but it seems I am not going to do it. I am dying, but in peace, happiness and serenity. We've worked for years as a cultural ambassador for Turkey and North of Cyprus. It is a fact that life is too short and time flies."

Hasan had been like a father to İbrahim, who was 18 when he left Cyprus and joined his brothers in Australia. He was reliant on his elder brother during his first year in Australia. Hasan was also the last person in their family to see their mother, Naciye, before she died. İbrahim's oldest brother, Ahmet, had passed away fifteen years ago, and his remaining sibling, Hasan, had passed away too. Although he had nephews, nieces, and a wide community, İbrahim felt terribly alone for the first time in many years.

The funeral service was held at the Sunshine Mosque in Victoria and hundreds attended the prayer service. *Zaman Australia* documented Hasan's final words and described the service[72] .

9/11 INTERFAITH SERVICE

On September 11, 2004, İbrahim entered the Sunshine mosque, ready to host an interfaith memorial program organised by the Australian Intercultural Society (AIS) for the victims of 9/11. Members of the press were present as well. İbrahim wanted to express the idea that there are other ways to battle terrorism besides attacking or occupying countries. "Violence leads to violence," he stated. Ironically, the majority of victims of terrorism are Muslims. According to Professor Rik Colsaet, Belgian Director of Security and Global Environment at the Royal Institute for International Relations, and author of *Al Qaeda, the Myth*, most victims of terrorism are Muslims.

---

[72] (Zafer Polat, August 3, 2000, *Zaman Australia*).

Professor Colsaet told *Today's Zaman* that out of the 175,000 victims of terrorism since 1990, only 4,000 are Westerners, including the September 11 victims[73].

The *Australian Associated Press* ran an article on September 11, 2004, entitled, "Muslim Leader Urges Compassion." It focused on how Muslims were being unfairly labelled as terrorists and were in danger of being punished for terrorist acts committed by a radical minority. İbrahim pointed out that history was repeating itself. He said, "Yesterday the baddies were communists, today they are someone else."

İbrahim was pleased that he had been quoted as saying, "A Muslim cannot be a terrorist and a terrorist cannot be a Muslim." It is a well-known statement made by Fethullah Gülen and was published in the *Washington Post* a day after the 9/11 terrorist attack.

The Age also quoted İbrahim stating that the Muslim community had been angered by those who killed in the name of Islam. He said, "It is not an Islamic practice. It is not done. You cannot take a life because you have not given a life. It is not up to us.[74]"

However, İbrahim was upset when a distorted representation of his viewpoint appeared in the newspaper. He had been quoted as saying, "Mr. Howard's foreign policies had 'invited terrorist attacks' and Australia should negotiate with terrorist organizations." İbrahim rejects this. "I had never said nor implied anything like that. I suggested that by sending armies to other countries, terrorism will not come to an end, and that there are other ways that must be used." This statement created controversy and was discussed and debated in Australia, Spain, China, and Singapore. Many believed that İbrahim was asking for compassion towards terrorists. İbrahim's statements were not retracted even after İbrahim contacted the newspaper.

---

[73] Selcuk Gultasli, 15 July, 2005 by Today's Zaman (English version of Turkish daily *Zaman Newspaper*)

[74] Agenzia Fides, 12 September, 2004 in *The Age*

HAJJ (PILGRIMAGE) IN 2005

One of İbrahim's most important goals in life was to make his obligatory pilgrimage to Mecca. In 2005, he finally made the trip he had eagerly desired. Although he had visited the holy land in the past outside of the time of Hajj, the major pilgrimage, he was filled with joy and excitement at being able to make the journey during the pilgrimage season.

The pilgrimage is both a physical and spiritual journey wherein a person seeks to purify past errors. As is the custom in the Muslim world, he asked for forgiveness from his friends and family members before departing on the journey.

Traveling in the holy land inspired him since he was following the footsteps of the Prophet Muhammad, peace be upon him, and His Companions. İbrahim recalled:

> I was extremely happy for being there. My grandfather, my parents, my aunts, and my older brothers greatly desired to go, but could not. I felt fortunate for being able to. I made dua for them while I was there. It was very crowded there, and despite being old, I was able to continue due to a special strength God granted me. While I was walking between the hills of Safa and Marwa[75], it felt like my feet weren't even touching the ground. I felt like I was flying. Nothing could express the spiritual happiness I felt at that

---

[75] Safa and Marwah are the two small hills in the precinct of the Ka'bah, Islam's holiest mosque. In Islamic tradition, Prophet İbrahim (Abraham) was commanded by God to leave his wife Hajar (Hagar) and their infant son Ismail (Ishmael) alone in the desert to test their faith. Although with difficulty, İbrahim obeyed God's command like all the other prophets. Hajar also accepted this command, despite her situation. When her basic provisions ran out, she began pacing frantically, and left Ismail to look for water or help nearby. She was going between the hills of Safa and Marwa, making sure to keep an eye on her son, and running back when she couldn't. She travelled between the hills seven times when she found that a spring of water sprouted near Ismail. The water is called Zamzam, and it continues to flow and quench the pilgrim's thirst. Going between the hills of Safa and Marwa was declared by Prophet Muhammad, peace be upon him, as a rite of pilgrimage (both Umrah and Hajj).

time. I didn't want to leave the vicinity of the Ka'bah. I had pains in my knees, and people made way for me to pass.

One day, when I was walking out of the Ka'bah, a stranger exchanged greetings with me and introduced himself. He invited me to his house for a meal. When I looked at his face, I saw a pure-hearted person. It felt like I had met him before. I didn't reject his offer and went to his home. He turned out to be a wealthy person. Someone else later told me that he would distribute food by full trucks to needy persons and pilgrims. The man told me, 'When I first saw you, I saw in your face a nobleness, humility, sincerity, and love. It seems like you come from a noble and blessed family.' Apparently, he was one of the wealthy men of the city. He offered me food and after eating I thanked him and left. I learnt that he also was a *Sayyid*.

İbrahim thanked the man graciously and went on his way. As to how that man was able to determine İbrahim's background is a mystery. In the Sufi tradition, there is a proverb, "There is a road from heart to heart." This explains how people may understand or love each other without verbal communication.

İbrahim continued, "On Mount Arafat, I saw the vision of the blessed men in white greeting me with smiles. The pleasant smell came to me again. None of my companions saw these men. I continued my worship there, prayed for my family and friends, and shed tears that flowed through my heart."

When İbrahim was in the Mosque of the Prophet in Medina, he heard a person calling after him, saying "Hamzah! Hamzah!" (Hamzah was the Prophet's uncle who protected the Prophet, died as a martyr when the Meccan polytheists attacked Medina, and is known and loved by all Muslims). İbrahim turned and saw a man calling out the name and coming towards him. When the man came close enough, he said in English, "Aren't you Hamzah?" İbrahim replied, "No." The man from Kosovo, who had a basic understanding of English, said, "You look like the actor (Anthony Quinn) who plays Hamzah in *The Message* film, which covers the life of Prophet Muhammad." A good conversation flowed from there in the holy mosque.

It was because of his resemblance to Anthony Quinn that İbrahim liked the actor. The fact that Anthony Quinn appeared in *The Message* and *Lion of the Desert* added to his appeal. İbrahim admired Quinn because he portrayed prominent Muslim historical figures convincingly. "To me, it was like he was sincere in his role and believed in whatever his character believed," said İbrahim. One of his favourite scenes in *The Message* is when a prominent Meccan man insults the Prophet and Hamzah (Quinn), the Prophet's uncle, strikes that Meccan saying, "Give them [Muslims] the right to express themselves freely." It was during the early stages of Islam when Quinn's character defended the Muslims. İbrahim said, "This is why I like Anthony Quinn. In my eyes, Anthony is still Hamzah."

Another tradition of Hajj pilgrims is to visit the gravesite of the martyrs of Uhud. Uhud is a mountain range where one of the major battles took place during the life of the Prophet. It was the second battle to defend the Muslim city of Medina. At Uhud, 70 Companions, including the Prophet's uncle, Hamzah, were killed. While İbrahim was visiting the gravesite, he saw turbaned horsemen passing by him and his companions. When he asked his companions, "Did you see the horsemen?" The companions raised their eyebrows, stating that they had not seen such a strange thing. At that point, İbrahim realized that he had experienced another vision.

İbrahim also visited the train station of the historical Ottoman Hijaz railway. At the station, he again saw the horsemen. Even though it is not permitted to take photos at the historical site, İbrahim snapped photos of the horsemen. To his surprise, none of the developed photos depicted horsemen. He concluded that the turbaned horsemen were the spirits of the Uhud martyrs. According to sacred sources of Islam (Qur'an and hadith), martyrs experience a different type of death. The martyr's spirit is still alive and able to visit the world from time to time with God's permission. İbrahim stated, "I have seen visions like these while awake and asleep during the difficult times in my life. When I saw the blessed faces smiling at me, I felt my burdens lighten. Later, I realized that this is a blessing of God, and that my duty is to offer sincere gratitude for these blessings."

İbrahim continued, "I loved Mecca and Medina so much that it hurt so much to leave those blessed lands. It felt as though I wanted to die there instead of leaving it. I had to leave, but that departure was very difficult on my soul. Despite the pain in my knees, I was able to complete my Hajj quite comfortably. I felt that this was a Divine blessing."

VISITING LARNACA AFTER DECADES

After returning from Hajj, İbrahim visited Larnaca in December of 2005. His heart felt heavy when he saw that his childhood homeland had undergone many changes. He visited the neighborhood where he had spent his childhood. His family home and the homes his neighbors were no longer there. The trees that took years to grow in his backyard had been destroyed. Their house was now owned by a Greek who sold firewood.

During İbrahim's childhood, there had been a spacious cotton field located behind the house. Now, houses dotted the landscape. He remained standing, gazing upon the unfamiliar structures. Memories of childhood events returned and tears began running down his face.

The street itself looked the same, but the buildings had either been renovated or torn down to make room for new buildings. İbrahim noted that the street's name, *Ikinci Selim Sokagi* (Selim II Street), had not been changed by the Greeks. Selim II (1524-1574) had been an Ottoman Sultan during the 16th century. İbrahim smiled at this.

İbrahim then visited his old school, the American Academy, which was still standing, but had undergone major alterations. The older buildings had been torn down. The school grounds were more extensive and trees stood where there had been no trees before. The entrance had changed altogether. "If there was no sign (indicating the school's name), it would be difficult for me to recognize it," said İbrahim. Since it was a Sunday, he could not enter the school grounds, and he had to be satisfied with having his picture taken along side the school gate. He stood by the gates, put his hands on the fence, and gazed into the school and into his past. He tried to recall the faces of his teachers and friends, and he remembered Ms. Fuller, the kind teacher who would advise him. He gazed upon the school grounds and recalled how he had raced around the track. Fifty-seven years had passed since he had graduated from the academy. He thought, "How time flies. How short life is."

İbrahim's next stop was the shrine of Hala Sultan. The orchards around the shrine had disappeared and were now plain fields. The once busy holy site had no other visitor while İbrahim was there. "It was like the place had been orphaned," he remarked. It was deprived of the children who played by the building, the visitors of different faiths who paid their respects, and the workers and fruit sellers who stopped by. He went to the mosque and prayed two *rakaat* (cycles of prayer) as a way of greeting the mosque, which is a tradition in Islam. After the prayer, he entered the room where Hala Sultan's grave lay and recited *Surah al-Fatiha*, the opening chapter of the Qur'an. He greeted Hala Sultan with "Assalamu alayka," the traditional Muslim greeting meaning, "Peace be with you." Then he turned to greet the Ottoman martyrs who were buried there as well after the Ottoman takeover of Cyprus.

It saddened him to see that the holy place had been neglected. He sat down. Childhood memories played before him. He watched his mother cooking food and guests being served. He saw children running about, feasting on the fruit provided by the local gardeners. The orchards belonged to the *awkaf* (foundation) of the shrine, so fruit would be given to visitors. In his mind's eye, İbrahim saw the caravans with horses carrying visitors to the shrine. The sound of the *muazzin* (the caller to prayer) rang in his ears. An image of a young İbrahim running until the child came to a lake arose in his mind.

He stood up and thought, "This world is nothing and meaningless. In a world where even the greatest of men and women die, it is not worth loving this world as though one were to live forever." Prophet

Muhammad, peace be upon him, said to Ibn 'Umar, one of his Companions, "Be in this world as though you were a stranger or a traveler" (Bukhari). Remembering this, İbrahim understood the truth behind those words.

THE ORDER OF AUSTRALIA

In 2007, İbrahim's name appeared on the Queen's Birthday Honours List and he became a member in the General Division of the Order of Australia, an award within the Australian Honours and Awards.

It was given for his service to the Islamic and Turkish communities of Australia, particularly through the establishment of educational facilities and settlement programs for immigrants, and the promotion of interfaith dialogue[76].

When *Zaman Australia* interviewed İbrahim after he had received the prestigious award, İbrahim had said, "My success is the community's success. In order to be successful, there needs to be teamwork. I would like to give my sincere thanks to those who stood by me. First, my wife, my daughters, my son-in-laws, Işık College administration, teachers, parents, and students, and the entire community. Also, I would like to thank Victorian Premier John Brumby, local members of Parliament, and town councilors."

In response, İbrahim received letters of gratitude from Governor-General Major General Michael Jeffrey, Governor of Victoria David de Krester, Premier of Victoria Steve Bracks, Minister for Immigration and Citizenship Kevin Andrews, US Consul General of Melbourne Earl M. Irving, Department of Immigration and Citizenship Secretary Andrew Metcalfe, and other politicians[77].

---

[76] Serkan Hussein and Edward Carusu, *Yesterday & Today: Turkish Cypriots of Australia*, p.104.

[77] "My success is the community's success," Zafer Polat, *Zaman Australia*, 18 June, 2007).

CHAPTER 10

A Living Archive

A LIVING ARCHIVE

O n the 29th of August, 2007, İbrahim attended a function sponsored by the National Archives of Australia (NAA). The National Archives had supported the publication of *"Uncommon Lives: Muslim Journeys,"* a compilation of material devoted to the history of Muslims in Australia. Using hundreds of records from its collection and locating many more documents, the NAA compiled a collective biography, which provides a glimpse into the times, the challenges early Muslims faced and the contribution they made to the nation. A digital archive of the 100-page feature, complete with pictures, letters, and government documents, is available online. The Department of Immigration and Citizenship provided financial support for the preparation of the online archive. An award-winning author, Hanifa Deen, whose grandfathers had immigrated to Australia from India, prepared the collection.

"Muslims were visiting Australia long before white settlement. By the 1700s, Macassans from Indonesia were sailing our northern shores, fishing for trepang and trading for pearls with the local Aboriginal people," observed Ross Gibbs, Director-General of the NAA. He added, "As a nation we owe a great deal to our Muslim settlers. It was their skills that enabled inland exploration of Australia, the establishment of the Western Australian goldfields and the expansion of the country's manufacturing industry."[78]

Senator Gary Humphrie delivered the opening speech at the NAA function and he emphasized the significance of this project as a part of Australia's national history. The senator congratulated Hanifa Deen for her efforts. Senator Humphrie stated that Hanifa Deen had

---

[78] http://www.naa.gov.au/about-us/media-releases/2007/muslim-lives-online.aspx

uncovered a "goldmine" of material and brought out a "cast of Muslim characters."

In a press release, the NAA wrote, "Attending the launch as a 'living archive' was İbrahim Dellal, a Turkish Cypriot who arrived in Australia in 1950 at the age of 18 and who became known and loved as a community leader and philanthropist. His cheerful enthusiasm helped establish mosques, Turkish schools, newspapers and community organisations." İbrahim was the final speaker of the night. Moreover, he was the only speaker and attendee who was also featured in *Uncommon Lives: Muslim Journeys*.

"When I first came, I had £50 in my pocket. Back then, people would come one at a time. There weren't groups coming together," İbrahim stated. The NAA recognized the support provided by earlier Muslim immigrants like İbrahim, together with government organizations, to the immigrants who came after 1968. İbrahim listed his activities in Australia, such as his efforts to unite the coalition of 17 Islamic organizations into a single entity, i.e., the Australian Federation of Islamic Societies (AFIS). He stated that Turkish immigrants contributed to Australia's development. He gave the example of Eastmeadows Işık College campus that had a 100% university enrolment rate that year, and maintained that it reflected the successful integration of Turks into Australian society[79].

VISITING GÜLEN IN 2007

In 2007, İbrahim and I were invited to speak at a retreat program near Lake Ontario in Canada. We both decided to use this opportunity to visit Gülen, who, at that time, was residing in a retreat centre in Pennsylvania.

The flight to Canada took nearly 26 hours. This gave me much time to talk with İbrahim and to listen as he described his life story. At that point, I realized that İbrahim was indeed a living archive and decided that his memories must be documented for future genera-

---

[79] Yeni Vatan, 3 September, 2007. Zaman, 3 September, 2007.

tions. His life story was attractive for many reasons. He was educated in Christian missionary schools and received the Jubilee Silver Medal from Queen Elizabeth II. In addition, he had served the Australian Muslim community for 57 years. He greatly admired Ottoman history and culture, and his character and stature was like that of an English lord. I discovered his spiritual dimension during that trip when he spoke about his visions, dreams, and blessed life.

When we were passing through customs in Los Angeles, I noticed that İbrahim was still with the customs officer. I collected our luggage, and came back to find him still carrying on a conversation with the customs officer. I was worried that something was wrong with his documents. All other passengers on the same flight had already cleared customs.

Another 15-20 minutes passed before he finally joined me. I asked him, "What was wrong?" He said, "The customs officer asked me what job I held in Australia, and I explained to him about the educational, cultural, and interfaith activities. I talked about the combination of secular and moral education. I spoke to him about the love of humanity and love in Islam. The officer said, 'Oh. I didn't know there were such things in Islam.' He kept asking questions, and even took notes. "He really liked what I said," İbrahim remarked.

At the retreat, İbrahim delivered several lectures to 200 attendees and described the history of the Ottoman Empire using Western sources. His audience was enthralled. He spoke about the history of Muslims in Australia as well. He focused on the struggles of Muslims in the fields of education and interfaith and intercultural dialogue. He described the founding of Işık Colleges in Victoria and Sule College in NSW, and the establishment of fifteen regional campuses. Over a ten-year period, İbrahim noted, the schools went from having a student body of 26 youngsters, educating nearly 4,000. He pointed out the success of the Eastmeadows and Upfield campuses in university enrolments in recent years and emphasized the role of countless volunteers who did not distinguish day from night when they offered their help nor hesitated when they signed their donation cheques.

During the lecture, İbrahim mentioned a meeting he had attended as a director of Işık College. This meeting was for the directors of the most successful schools in Victoria. One director asked him, "How did your school go from rags-to-riches in ten years?" Most of the other schools had a long history and larger budgets due to high tuition costs (eight times greater than Işık College's tuition). İbrahim smiled and said, "Well, first we believed, and we worked hard. We struggled against hardship. We didn't despair, and by God's will, we did it."

İbrahim's words were received well by the women attending the retreat, especially when İbrahim talked about the woman's importance and role in the family. He repeated his mother's words, "When you educate a girl, you educate a whole family." About the woman's role in the family, he said:

> The strength of the Muslim Turk is the family. And the strength of the family is the woman. The woman's life and strength is her man. The family's life and strength, lasting happiness, peace, and health is in the woman. The one who continues and protects the family is the man.

> The family is humanity's happiness, peace, security, health, trust, and positive life and blessing. If there is no family, there is no unity, no blessing, no community, and no government.

> Therefore, the Ottomans, and the Muslim Turk's strength is the family. And the one who unites the family, gives compassion, continues its lasting health and peace is the true Turkish Muslim woman. And the protector and continuer of this foundation is the true Turkish Muslim man

During the question-answer session, İbrahim was asked, "How do you answer Westerners who ask you about the hijab?"[80] İbrahim replied, "I tell them, 'It's a matter of privacy. When a woman covers, she is keeping herself private and not public.'

---

80   Hijab is the Arabic word for "covering." Based on Qur'anic and hadith sources, it is required for women to cover their entire bodies except their hands and face. It does not apply to only the headscarf, but to dressing modestly.

İbrahim also described Australia and emphasized that it is a beautiful country, accepting of Muslims and full of opportunity. Australia granted citizenship to Muslims, and now Muslims were taking advantage of the opportunities in Australia and entering into different areas in government, business, sports, and education. He praised the Australian government for educational funding to private schools, which did not occur in the US or in Canada. "We are very lucky to be in Australia," he said. "Plus, the weather is good. It's not cold like it is here." He encouraged the audience members to visit Australia and see the unusual native fauna.

From the retreat center in Canada, İbrahim and the author traveled by car to Niagara Falls. İbrahim gazed upon the falls and said, "I heard and read about it, but did not know how amazing it was. It is really amazing." The snow began falling in heavy flakes after we departed from Canada. We should have arrived in Pennsylvania by 8pm, but the snow was so heavy that the driver reduced his speed to 25 miles per hours (from the 60 miles per hour average speed). It was midnight when we arrived at the retreat centre in Pennsylvania.

In the morning, we breakfasted with Gülen. Gülen had not forgotten İbrahim. İbrahim was amazed since he had only spent a few days with Gülen in Australia fifteen years ago. Indeed, Gülen is a man who meets with hundreds of people every month. Gülen treated İbrahim with special care. Despite the fact that Gülen was ill at the time, Gülen came up to our room to see us on our second day there. He spoke with İbrahim, and it wasn't long before both were in tears reminiscing about their past pains and pleasures. They were kindred souls. Before we left, Gülen gave İbrahim a silk prayer mat and said, "I only prayed on this once." İbrahim was overjoyed that he had something from *Hoca Efendi* that he can remember him by. We said our farewells to Hoca Efendi, and left, wishing we could have stayed longer.

During our return trip, I was able to ask İbrahim questions and listen to him speak of his active past. Because of his relatively advanced age, he could not immediately recall spefici details of his; however, as I asked him questions, his memories slowly emerged.

Back in Melbourne, when İbrahim showed the prayer mat to his wife, Sheila, and expressed his desire to pray on it, Sheila replied, "Since this is the prayer mat *Hoca Efendi* prayed on, let's hang it on the wall as a memento."

INTERFAITH SERVICE FOR BUSHFIRE VICTIMS AT SUNSHINE MOSQUE

In one of Australia's deadliest bushfires, over 200 people and countless animals lost their lives in the Victorian bushfires of 2009. More than 2,000 homes and 35,000 structures were destroyed and thousands more were damaged. 7,500 were left homeless[81]. Together with the board members of the mosque, the Australian Intercultural Society (AIS) organized an interfaith prayer service for the bushfire victims. Leading religious figures, such as Catholic Archbishop Denis Hart, attended the service. It was the 22nd of February in 2009 when İbrahim welcomed the believers with a warm speech. He stated:

> Dear Sisters, Brothers, Neighbours, and Friends,
>
> Once again, destiny brings us together. It gives me great pleasure to extend our warmest welcome to you all. Assalamu alaikum (Peace be with you). Our mosque is a place of worship for us all. We unite five times a day in the presence of Allah and pray for peace and harmony for us all. Mosques bring us together and unite us. We accept each other as equals and remember our responsibilities toward each other.
>
> Remember that as human beings we are answerable to Allah for all our actions, words, and deeds. As always, we shall work and pray to strengthen the bonds of friendship and continue to meet all challenges together. Working together leads us to achieve success, peace, harmony, and happiness. It is happiness to do right, to be just, live a healthy way of life, and set the best possible examples as human beings. Happiness and success is achieved by being sincere, working together, accepting and respecting, learning from

---

[81] Sydeny Morning Herald, 11 Feb, 2009

each other and about each other, and building the bridges of trust, compassion, caring, and sharing. Love is trust.

Peace, harmony, and security belong to freedom, not fear or restricting others. The freedom of others is a branch of our own freedom. When one's freedom is restricted, our own freedom is restricted. We are many, but we are one. We are one family, the family of Abraham, peace be upon him. We shall continue to do right, and oppose wrong. Human beings have three major enemies: ignorance, poverty, and hate. We shall continue to work for valued education, compassion, caring, and sharing. Love, do not hate and oppose wrong.

Dear sisters and brothers, it is important that we always remember that life is short and our time is limited. Human beings have no time to quarrel, but we have very little time to do good things, and please the Maker and the Master, Allah. May Allah shower His blessings upon us all. May Allah give us all the strength to do right an dbe just, and live and let live in peace and harmony. Insha Allah (God willing), SubhanAllah (Glory to God), Alhamdulillah (Praise is to God), Allahu Akbar (God is the Greatest).

We pray for those whose died and those who have been devastated by the recent bushfires. We offer our sincere condolences. Once again, our warmest welcome to you all. Thank you for coming.

THREE IMPORTANT PRINCIPLES

It's not only events like these that draw people's attention to Ibrahim. He has been interviewed by newspaper reporters, broadcasters, and academic researchers for his memoroies of life in Australia before the 1970s and many of the community projects he was involved in. This has not been the first attempt to document İbrahim's life and achievements. Hüseyin Duru also began to write a memoir in Turkish; however, the book has yet to be published. The book's name is "*Dunyanin Dibi Tarih Oluyor* (The Bottom of the World is Becoming History)". In this book, İbrahim explains his life philosophy and gives advice to leaders:

> From what I remember, my forefathers focused on three things. If a person, community, or state wants to be productive, these three principles are a must.

First: The human mind must be satisfied. This is a must. A person's whole world must appeal to his or her mind. During stormy times, the mind should be able to say, "This is my path" and not be swept away.

Second: The human appetite must be satisfied. Poverty leads to crimes and disunity.

Third: Security must be established and maintained. This means law. The laws must be clear and enforced upon everyone equally. You must ensure everyone's security and take precautions in this aspect.

These three things are important. We have not been able to do these (in recent centuries as Muslims). A good education decreases poverty and increases security. A place without security is full of jealousy, corruption, and enmity. We must live and keep alive these three principles.

The strength of the Muslim Turk is the family. And the strength of the family is the woman. The woman's life and strength is her man. The family's life and strength, lasting happiness, peace, and health is in the woman. The one who continues and protects the family is the man.

The Ottoman Empire's and today's Muslim Turk's foundation is the family. The family's foundation and continuation is the Turkish Muslim woman. The one who directs, satisfies, and protects the family is the Turkish Muslim man.

The family is humanity's happiness, peace, security, health, trust, and positive life and blessing. If there is no family, there is no unity, no blessing, no community, and no government.

Therefore, the Ottomans, and the Muslim Turk's strength is the family. And the one who unites the family, gives compassion, continues its lasting health and peace is the true Turkish Muslim woman. And the protector and continuer of this foundation is the true Turkish Muslim man.

Today, they are working to destroy the family through various ploys and schemes, and under various names, knowingly or unknowingly.

What are these plans?

The quickest is TV, internet, etc. When these media are used for positive and beneficient things, they are very beneficial. It is important that we always research and be careful. Are these mediums, films, with their words and pictures, beneficial or negative, do they establish or destroy, are they auspicious or destructive?

Just like they were around yesterday, there are also schemes under various names designed to weaken and wreck the family life.

UNTIL HIS FINAL BREATH

At the age of 78, İbrahim continues to commute from Ivanhoe to Eastmeadows where his office is located on the Işık College Girls' Campus. He is there six days a week, volunteering not only as the honorary president of the Selimiye Foundation, but also devoting much time and energy to educational, cultural, spiritual, and inter-faith activities. His every act echoes his passion for serving others.

Sixty years ago, İbrahim arrived on the shores of Australia prepared for his new life. He spoke English and was familiar with Western culture as a result of his education at the American Academy and British Institute of Technology in Larnaca. He understood the reasoning behind the Western system. İbrahim believes that, "if you don't know how to use the system, the system will use you and finish you." He used his knowledge and experience not only to further himself, but also to help establish the Turkish and Muslim communities in Australia.

Together with the Australian Federation of Islamic Councils (AFIC), İbrahim aided the Australian economy with the boost in halal meat and livestock export to Muslim countries such as Iran and the Gulf States. For three years he was in charge of the halal meat committee for the AFIC. He worked to establish contacts and formed business connections with international traders. The export business continues to flourish and has generated billions of dollars in revenue for Australian businesses.

Despite his obvious achievements, humility is at the base of İbrahim's character. The closest people to İbrahim all spoke about his humility, and mentioned that it increased their respect for him. His humility was often a source of inspiration. When İbrahim would be complimented on this aspect of his character, he would often reply, "Humility is a requirement of my faith."[82] İbrahim would not advertise his achievements or speak of the medal he received from the Queen in public, and rarely discussed his achievements in private. Instead, he used his medal as a credential to further his goals, especially when he was interacting with politicians and bureaucrats.

Dr. Abdul Khaliq Kazi said, "İbrahim never quit and left. He never just sat at home. İbrahim never divorced himself from the community." From observing İbrahim for two years and writing his biography, I believe that serving the community is as natural and necessary to İbrahim as breathing air. As İbrahim said, "If I don't do this, I will die. It is a part of my life, and I will do this until my last breath."

---

82 As in other religions, humility is a part of Islamic faith and practice. "And *the servants of (Allah) Most Gracious are those who walk on the earth in humility, and when the ignorant address them, they say, 'Peace!'*" (Qur'an 25:63). Abu Huraira reported Allah's Messenger as saying: Charity does not in any way decrease the wealth and the servant who forgives Allah adds to his respect, and the one who shows humility Allah elevates him in the estimation (of the people). [Sahih Muslim 32: 6264]